GW01564153

CREDITS

Groove Alchemy
by Stanton Moore

Edited by Joe Bergamini

Design and Layout by Rick Gratton

Cover by Kenneth Robin

Executive Producers: Paul Siegel and Rob Wallis

Photos by Dino Perucci and Allison Murphy

Photos on pages 1, 2, and 5 by Maureen Brown

Photos on page 10 by Paul LaRaia

Photo on page 34 by Clayton Call

Music Engraving by Rick Gratton

Text Editing by Jill Flomenhoft

Additional Editing by Paul Siegel

Audio tracks recorded at The Dugout
Engineered by Mike Napolitano

Catalog HDBK25/HL6620147
ISBN: 9781423475163

ACKNOWLEDGMENTS

The research for this book came from the following books:

Jim Payne's *Give The Drummers Some!* (re-issued as *The Great Drummers of R&B, Funk & Soul*) Allan Slutsky and Chuck Silverman's *The Funkmasters* and Zoro's *The Commandments Of R&B Drumming*.

Additional information came from the following liner notes:

James Brown's *Star Time*, written by James Brown, Cliff White, Harry Weinger, Nelson George and Alan Leeds, and *Funk Power*, written by Alan Leeds.

Some further information also came from good old oral history.

I'd like to acknowledge the drummers whose grooves and playing I have learned from and who inspired me to write this book. If you're not familiar with these guys yet, make sure you check them out: Zigaboo Modeliste, Clyde Stubblefield, Jabo Starks, Melvin Parker, Idris Muhammad, James Black, Bernard Purdie, Al Jackson Jr., Roger Hawkins, David Garibaldi, Clayton Fillyau, Mike Clark, John Bonham, Brian Blade, Johnny Vidacovich, Herlin Riley, Shannon Powell, Russell Batiste, Herman Ernest, Levon Helm, Willie Green, Geoff Clapp, Raymond Weber, Jeffery Alexander, Adam Deitch, Kevin O'Day, Joe Russo, Carlo Nuccio, and Johnny Thomassie.

INSIDE THIS BOOK

Born and raised in New Orleans, Stanton Moore is a dedicated drummer and performer especially connected to the city, its culture and collaborative spirit. Driven and inspired by the thriving music scene of his hometown—which includes such greats as Professor Longhair, Doctor John and The Meters—Moore's name is now mentioned amongst these Big Easy mainstays.

In the early '90s, Moore helped found the New Orleans-based funk band Galactic, with whom he has recorded seven albums and toured the world, performing nearly 200 gigs a year. Stanton has also released several critically acclaimed albums as a leader: *All Kooked Out!* (1998), *Flyin' the Koop* (Verve/Blue Thumb)(2001), *III* (Telarc)(2006), *Emphasis!* (*on parenthesis*) (2008), as well as the forthcoming companion album to this book, *Groove Alchemy*. He is also co-founder of Garage a Trois, with whom he has recorded four albums.

An active educator, Stanton has appeared worldwide performing at drum clinics, masterclasses, and festivals. Stanton's *Take It To The Street* (Carl Fischer) series of two DVDs and a book is considered a worldwide educational standard on New Orleans drumming styles. He has been a contributing writer for *Drum!*, *Modern Drummer*, and *Downbeat* magazines, and has been featured on the cover of more than 6 drum publications. In 2005, he launched a signature line of cymbals with Bosphorus Cymbals and a signature drumstick with the Vic Firth stick company. In 2009, Moore formed his own company to market his signature titanium snare drum.

An extremely versatile drummer, Moore has recorded with Corrosion of Conformity, Irma Thomas, Robert Walter, Tom Morello and Boots Riley, Will Bernard, Diane Birch, and Alec Ounsworth, and has performed with John Scofield, Karl Denson, George Porter Jr. and Leo Nocentelli (of the Meters), Charlie Hunter, Warren Haynes, John Medeski and Chris Wood (of Medeski, Martin and Wood), Donald Harrison Jr., Dr. Lonnie Smith, Dr. John, Tab Benoit, Robert Walter, the New Orleans Klezmer All-Stars, the Preservation Hall Jazz Band, and others.

Deeply affected by Katrina and its aftermath, New Orleans' native son was quick to lend a hand by spearheading Tipitina's Music Workshop: free seminars that cater to children, with a rotating cast of well-known professionals to promote the preservation of New Orleans music. Stanton and his wife Aletta also set up the Staletta Fund, a scholarship for aspiring music students. Moore is also involved with the New Orleans charities Gulf Restoration Network, Voice of the Wetlands All-Stars, and the Roots of Music.

www.stantonmoore.com

www.myspace.com/stantonmoore

GROOVE ALCHEMY

INTRODUCTION

"Here's a tune I want to do. It's a slow 12/8 but I don't want to do it like that. I'm not sure what I want to do with it. Go to the drums and try to come up with an approach for this tune. I'll stay here in the control room and I'll tell you when I hear something I like." That's what Irma Thomas said to me in the studio while working on her Grammy winning record *After the Rain*. Irma, the producer, two engineers, and the entire band were all waiting for me to come up with an idea. We're in a nice (read: not cheap) studio and the clock is ticking. Irma is a great singer and the Queen of New Orleans Soul. I've been listening to her since I was born, and she is one of my parents' favorite artists. You know the Rolling Stones' "Time Is On My Side"? Irma sang the original version. All that said, of course I wanted to do a good job, and I wanted Irma to be happy. So I went in and started playing some ideas I had, and I started modifying them for the tune. I changed out my bass drum, experimented with different sticks, rods, and blasticks, and I tried some different tunings on several snare drums. In a few minutes I had something Irma was happy with and we had a new direction for the tune. I was able to do this because I have a deep catalog of ideas and grooves which I can draw from and modify, even when placed in the hot seat.

Many times I have been in the studio or working on music with an artist or a group of musicians to find we are all reaching for a common goal. We are all trying to make the work we are creating turn out the best it can, and hopefully others will find it good or even great. Sometimes though, reaching our collective goal can prove challenging and may even seem unattainable. I constantly make adjustments to what I am doing at the drums to help make the music better. Sometimes I choose to make these adjustments myself, and sometimes I am asked to make certain adjustments. Sometimes these adjustments are relatively straightforward and simple, like "Could you change that snare drum?", "Could you dampen that bass drum some more?", or "Could you go to the ride for the chorus?" But sometimes these adjustments require experimentation and even a bit of guesswork. I've been asked, "Could you swing what you are doing a bit less and play straighter?", "Could you change the beat you are playing?", or "Here's a demo of a tune; I don't want to do it anything like this, but I'm not sure exactly how I want to do it. Go out there and play some stuff and I'll tell you if I like any of it."

My intention in writing this book is to present my approach to groove playing from a creative point of view. While we'll cover some history and background, I'd like to primarily focus on ways you can combine different styles and methods to come up with new grooves. We'll examine many nuances and details and through a deeper understanding of these finer points, you'll discover new ways to improve your groove. You'll learn how to fine-tune your playing and improve what it is you are doing. I'm hoping that by working with these concepts, you will eventually be able to mine your own resources and learn how to turn your grooves into musical gold.

A groove is often described as what happens when two or more people lock into each other and the music at hand in a way that transcends just playing the notes. A good groove can make a whole room full of people suddenly want to move. This is a very powerful thing to witness, and even more powerful when you are actually involved in the groove and the music moving the people.

Even though a "groove" is usually created by two or more people and a "beat" is usually created with the drums by themselves, I like the term *groove* more than *beat* and will be calling a lot of the "beats" in this book "grooves." I suppose my terminology is also a result of my hope that the beats in this book will be used to create new grooves and move new masses of people.

INTRODUCTION

While my first book, *Take It To The Street,* presented my approach to the many aspects of New Orleans drumming, this book is intended to explore my approach to funk and other types of groove drumming. This book can in many ways be seen as a continuation of *Take It To The Street.*

There are many classic grooves transcribed throughout, and while I encourage learning these as faithfully as possible, I also suggest using them as tools to create new grooves as well. By understanding what has already been done, we can better understand how to progress forward.

You may want to consider some suggestions for ways to use this book. I suggest listening to the audio by itself to further internalize the feel of a lot of these grooves.

Also, you may want to try copping the grooves by ear first. Try coming up with your own variations based on your first impressions of what you hear. Remember to *record or notate* what you play. You can always go back and learn the grooves note for note, but you can't always recapture the inspiration you get from hearing something for the first time.

ABOUT THE AUDIO

The Online audio contains the tracks for this book. Using the access code on the card in the back of the book, you can listen to the tracks online or download them to your device. PLAYBACK+, a multi-functional audio player, allows you to slow down audio without changing pitch and set loop points.

INTRODUCTION

PRACTICING WITH THIS BOOK

I suggest practicing slowly and precisely, with a good feel. I also suggest practicing these grooves to a metronome. I've found it helpful when learning new material to set the metronome to a reasonable tempo and start playing the groove at hand. You may be able to play the first few notes okay and then the rest of the groove may give you trouble. Try adding each note after you have the preceding notes down. You can add one sixteenth note at a time if you have to. Keep adding to that first bit until you have the whole groove down.

You may also want to try getting comfortable with one limb at a time. For example, once you understand the right hand, add the left hand. Once the hands are comfortable, try adding the bass drum foot.

Remember to have fun, get creative, and stay funky. I hope you enjoy this material.

Stanton Moore

DRUM KEY

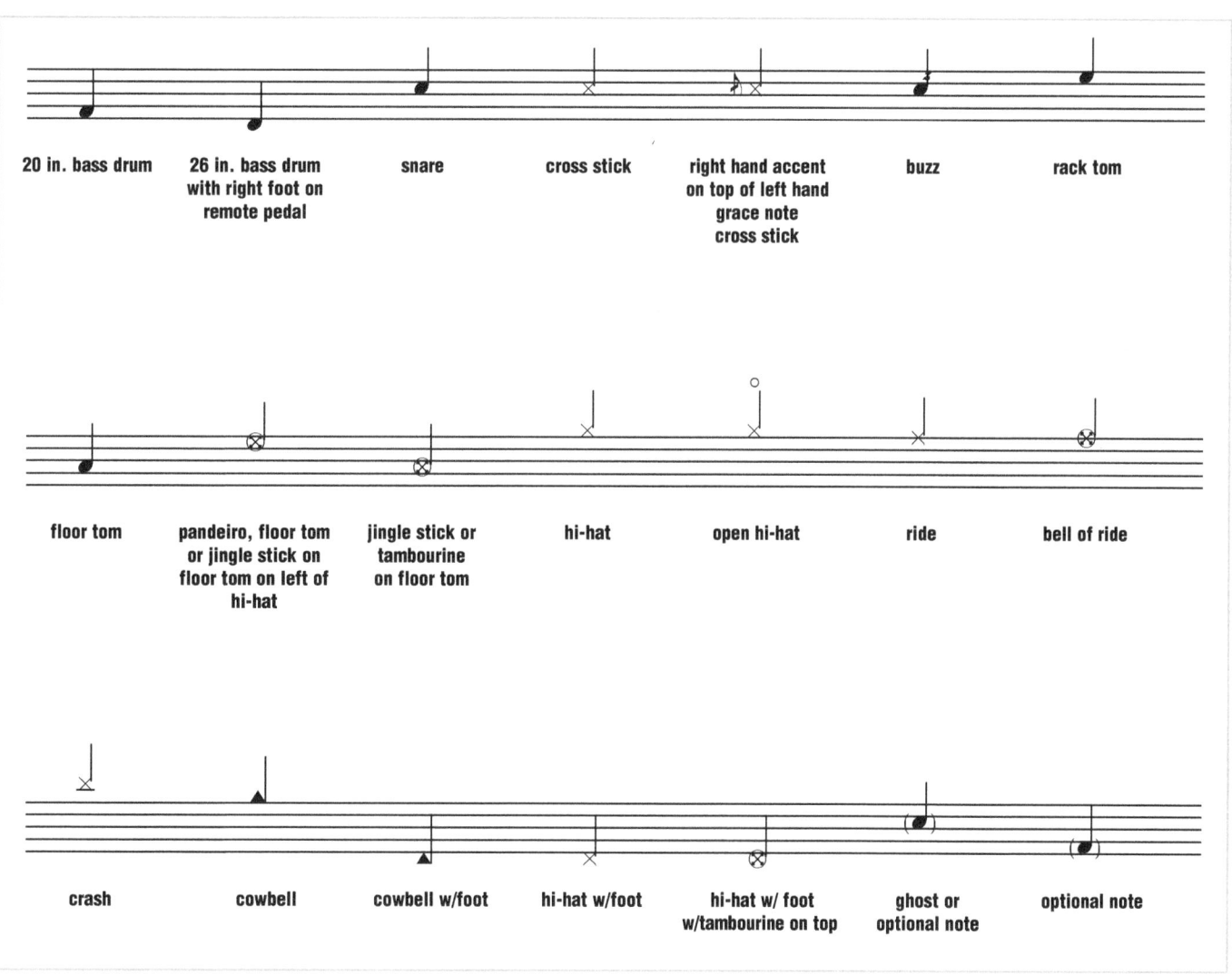

Clyde Stubblefield

John "Jabo" Starks

THE ROOTS OF FUNK

EXAMINING THE ROOTS OF FUNK

In this section we'll take a look at some of the early developments of funk drumming and where some of the modern funk drumming vocabulary came from. While this book will cover some historical background, it is not intended to be a historical account. Some great books that focus on the history and background of funk drumming include Jim Payne's *Give The Drummers Some!* (re-issued as *The Great Drummers of R&B, Funk & Soul*), Allan Slutsky and Chuck Silverman's *The Funkmasters,* and Zoro's *The Commandments of R&B Drumming.* I suggest checking them out if you want to develop an even deeper understanding of funk and groove drumming.

I'd like to get started by going right to the source: the grooves of James Brown. As I've said, there has been a good deal written about this subject already, but I would like to consider some of the nuances and details of some of the most important grooves to come out of the James Brown catalog. While I'd like to concentrate primarily on the drumming of John "Jabo" Starks and Clyde Stubblefield, let's first take a look at the history of the earlier important James Brown drummers and grooves.

Before we get started, let's check out a track

1. "Squash Blossom" FULL MIX (Introductory Track)

A BRIEF HISTORY OF JAMES BROWN'S DRUMMERS

Nat Kendrick joined James Brown's band in 1959 and was his first drummer of note. He played on most of Brown's early recordings.

In 1962 **Clayton Fillyau** joined the band and played on the legendary *Live at the Apollo* record. Kendrick stuck around and continued to play on some of the recordings, and Brown himself played on some of the recordings during this early period as well.

In addition to *Live at the Apollo*, Fillyau recorded some pivotal tunes with Brown. He contributed some powerful rhythmic innovations, namely "I've Got Money" and the live version of "Signed, Sealed and Delivered."

In 1964 **Melvin Parker** joined Brown's band after being pursued for some time. Parker agreed to come on board on the condition that he could bring aboard his brother Maceo on saxophone. Melvin Parker recorded "Out of Sight," "Papa's Got a Brand New Bag," and "I Got You (I Feel Good)."

In 1966 **John "Jabo" Starks** was finally wooed away from Bobby "Blue" Bland's band and joined up with Brown. A couple of months later, **Clyde Stubblefield** joined as well. Stubblefield recorded the hit "Cold Sweat" and opened up a new world of what was possible for James Brown and his band, both musically and success-wise. During the next few years Clyde recorded "I Got the Feelin'," "Say it Loud—I'm Black and I'm Proud," "Soul Pride," "Mother Popcorn," "Funky Drummer," "Since You've Been Gone," and a killing remake of "Give it Up Or Turnit a Loose."

In 1970 Brown's band, unhappy with their working situation, left to go out on their own. Jabo Starks, being a loyal band member (and signed to a contract), decided to stay on. A group of teenagers from Cincinnati were recruited to be Brown's new band. Brown had ties to Cincinnati because his record label, King, was located there. The New J.B.'s, as they were called, were headed by bassist William "Bootsy" Collins and his guitar-playing brother Phelps "Catfish" Collins. Brown brought his New J.B.'s into the studio and came out with "Sex Machine." Pleased with the success of this new formula, Brown rushed the band back into the studio and came out with "Super Bad," "Talkin' Loud and Sayin' Nothing," and "Soul Power." The Collins boys moved on a year later, but Jabo stuck around and in 1974 recorded "The Payback" and "Papa Don't Take No Mess." On the latter, a rejoined Maceo Parker plays (in my opinion) the funkiest four bars of saxophone ever recorded.

Note: For a more in-depth history of the great James Brown drummers, check out Jim Payne's *Give The Drummers Some!* (re-issued as *The Great Drummers of R&B, Funk & Soul*).

JAMES BROWN

In 1962 Clayton Fillyau recorded "I've Got Money." Fillyau came up with this beat after spending some time with the drummer for New Orleans piano player Huey "Piano" Smith. Fillyau met this drummer (believed to be either Charles "Hungry" Williams or Joseph "Smokey" Johnson) while Huey Smith's band was touring through Fillyau's hometown of St. Petersburg, Florida. Fillyau then took some of the syncopation he was shown, distinctive of most New Orleans drumming, and blended it with some aspects of the drum cadences he learned while attending Florida A&M. He came up with this groove and put it to James Brown's song "I've Got Money."

2. "I've Got Money" intro 1962, drums: Clayton Fillyau, c. 162 bpm.

3. "I've Got Money" main groove.

Many people consider this beat to be the seed of the "James Brown beat" and the spark that ignited the flame of funk. Notice that the unusually bright tempo of this song makes this track sound very similar to the drum & bass beats that came more than 30 years later.

Also note the similarities between this groove and the groove to the New Orleans classic "Big Chief." Even though "Big Chief" was released after "I've Got Money," the beat to "Big Chief" is the stuff that New Orleans drummers had been playing for a long time. It's highly probable that "Hungry" Williams or Smokey Johnson showed Fillyau something very close to this beat.

4. "Big Chief" Professor Longhair 1964, drums: Smokey Johnson, c. 130 bpm.

Right hand on rim or side of floor tom.

JAMES BROWN

Now, for fun let's blend these two grooves together.

5. "Big Chief," "I've Got Money" combo.

Try to play this in the range of 100-162 bpm.

Fillyau's innovations lit a fire in the James Brown camp. Not one to be outdone, James Brown (who liked to play drums on his own songs from time to time) came up with this groove to "Limbo Jimbo" in 1962.

6. "Limbo Jimbo" 1962, drums: James Brown, c. 112 bpm.

Nat Kendrick then came up with the following groove for "Soul Food, Parts 1 & 2" in 1963. Notice some similarities in the accent structure of this beat to "Limbo Jimbo"? This beat foreshadows many beats to come with its displaced backbeats, active grace notes, and buzzes.

7. "Soul Food, Parts 1 & 2" 1963, drums: Nat Kendrick, c. 123 bpm.

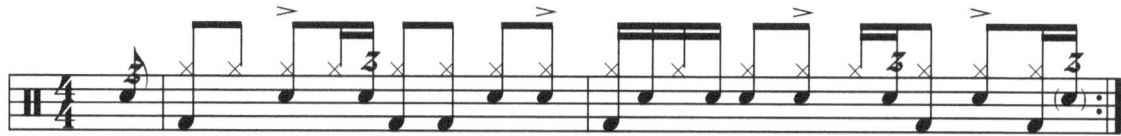

In 1963 Clayton Fillyau played this beat for a live version of Brown's "Signed, Sealed and Delivered." Notice the similarities in the accent structure of this groove and Clyde Stubblefield's groove to "I Got the Feelin'."

8. "Signed, Sealed and Delivered" 1963, drums: Clayton Fillyau, c. 158 bpm

JAMES BROWN

In 1964, Melvin Parker recorded "Out Of Sight," and in 1965 he recorded "Papa's Got A Brand New Bag" and "I Got You (I Feel Good)." He introduced a clean, stripped-down style that utilized the cross-stick (or rim click) technique on the snare and, with "Brand New Bag" and "I Feel Good", the recurring open hi-hat on the & of 1 and the & of 3. This opening of the hi-hat on the &'s of 1 and 3 creates a "shoop" that sets up the backbeat for a crisp snap. This development has appeared many times since (especially in the drumming of Jabo Starks), and continues to appear in great grooves to this day.

9. "Out Of Sight" 1964, drums: Melvin Parker, c. 130 bpm.

10. "Papa's Got A Brand New Bag" 1965, drums: Melvin Parker, c. 127 bpm.

11. "I Got You (I Feel Good)" 1965, drums: Melvin Parker, c. 147 bpm.

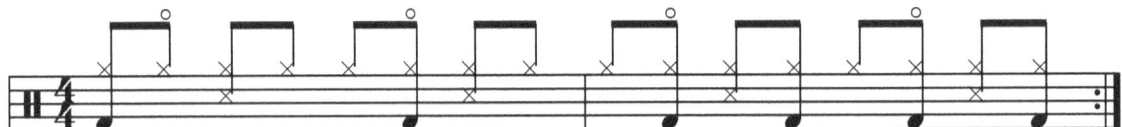

In 1966 James Brown was so glad to finally have wooed Jabo Starks away from Bobby "Blue" Bland that he recorded a tune with Jabo and named it after his new drummer. Notice the similarities to Fillyau's beat on "I've Got Money"?

12. "Jabo" 1966, drums: John "Jabo" Starks, c. 128 bpm.

JAMES BROWN

When Clyde Stubblefield joined the band, Fillyau was still around—driving the bus, actually. So, Fillyau taught Clyde the show. When Clyde Stubblefield recorded "Cold Sweat" in 1967, he utilized several of the innovations from the drummers that preceded him to come up with this masterpiece. He used the displaced backbeat idea pioneered by James Brown, Nat Kendrick, and Clayton Fillyau, and incorporated the open hi-hat on the & of 1 and the & of 3 originated by Melvin Parker. Genius? Yes. Pulled out of the sky? No.

13. "Cold Sweat" 1967, drums: Clyde Stubblefield, c. 112 bpm.

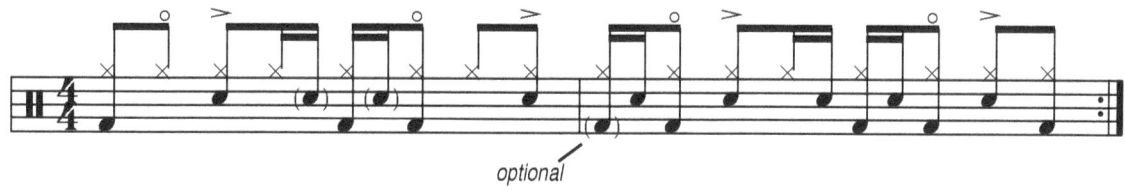

optional

In 1968 Clyde really outdid himself with "I Got the Feelin'." Again he used the displaced backbeats and recurring open hi-hat, but this time he unveiled his secret weapon: three repeating sixteenth notes in the left hand with an accent sometimes in the middle. This Stubblefield original rears its challenging head in several of his grooves to follow.

Also note that the rhythmic structure is very similar to Clayton Fillyau's groove to "Signed, Sealed and Delivered." In this tune Clyde plays a lot of subtle variations, but here's the main groove that he settles into. We'll examine this groove more deeply in the following chapter.

14. "I Got the Feelin'" 1968, drums: Clyde Stubblefield, c. 128 bpm.

Also in 1968, Jabo comes up with this interesting groove to "Licking Stick-Licking Stick." Notice again the similarity to Fillyau's "I've Got Money," but this time Jabo utilizes Melvin Parker's cross-sticks and recurring open hi-hat on the upbeats of 1 and 3.

15. "Licking Stick-Licking Stick" 1968, drums: John "Jabo" Starks, c. 105 bpm.

JAMES BROWN

Still in 1968, Stubblefield came up with "Say It Loud—I'm Black And I'm Proud" and "Soul Pride." With these two, Clyde introduces another innovation, the quarter-note hi-hat pattern.

16. **"Say It Loud–I'm Black And I'm Proud"** **1968, drums: Clyde Stubblefield, c. 113 bpm.**

I've transcribed the first four bars here, but notice that the majority of the song is based on five-bar phrases. Also note that Clyde's groove in the bridge is directly related to the 3-2 clave.

First 4 bars:

17. **"Soul Pride, Parts 1 & 2"** **1968, drums: Clyde Stubblefield, c. 128 bpm.**

GROOVE ALCHEMY

JAMES BROWN

Let's also check out Clyde's killer 18-bar break in "Soul Pride." There are a lot of challenging chatter note passages within this break. It's also interesting to note that this break (along with Gregory Sylvester "G.C." Coleman's break in the Winstons' "Amen Brother") is the basis for a lot of drum & bass beats. DJs began speeding up and cutting up this break and the "Amen" break to form the foundation for drum & bass. While the original break is in the 132 bpm range, drum & bass is usually sped up to the 160-180 bpm range.

18. "Soul Pride" **break 1968, drums: Clyde Stubblefield, c. 132 bpm.**

JAMES BROWN

Here's another one of Clyde's quarter-note hi-hat grooves. This is the groove to 1969's "Mother Popcorn."

19. "Mother Popcorn" 1969, drums: Clyde Stubblefield, c. 116 bpm.

Here are some things I came up with to work on Clyde's three-note phrases. Try these with eighth notes on the hi-hat, à la "I Got the Feelin'" and the break of "Soul Pride."

20. c. 118 bpm

21.

22.

23.

24.

JAMES BROWN

25.

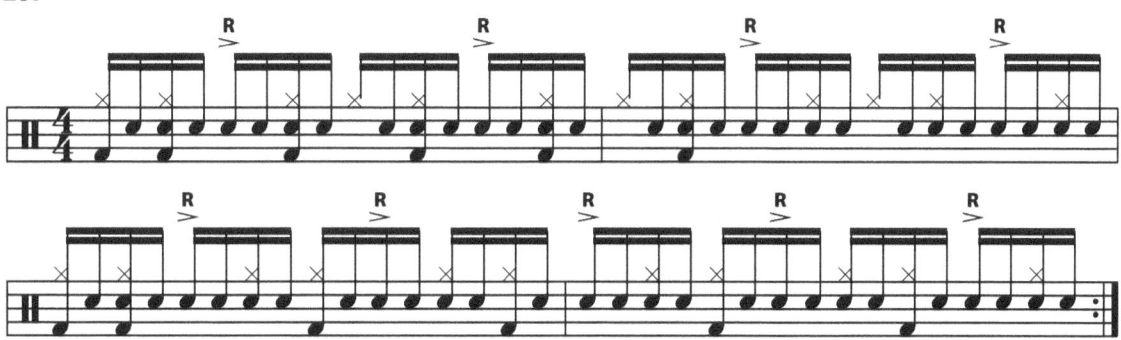

Here's one that isolates the repeating three-across-four phrase Clyde utilizes in the bridge of "I Got the Feelin'" and in the break of "Soul Pride."

26.

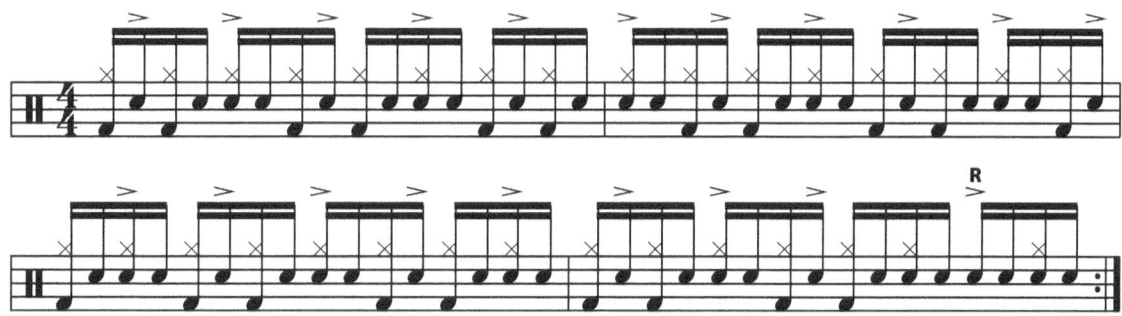

And here's one that works on the three-chatter-note phrase in the left hand with quarter notes in the right hand, á la "Say It Loud," "Mother Popcorn," and the main groove of "Soul Pride."

27.

JAMES BROWN

In 1969 Clyde also recorded the masterpiece "Funky Drummer." Clyde begins the tune with a very simple sixteenth-note hi-hat groove with a missing 1 on the bass drum. He gradually morphs the groove into an eight-bar break that is one of the most sampled drum breaks of all time, with the "Amen Brother" break maybe coming close. I've transcribed the whole eight-bar break. Usually only bar 1 or bar 3 is sampled, due to vocals present in the rest of the break. Depending on which bar is sampled, you may have heard the (slightly) open hi-hat in different places. The consistent sixteenth notes in the right hand along with all the other intricacies between the snare and bass drum make this a very challenging break to play. I've heard speculation that this tune (like "Papa's Got A Brand New Bag") may originally have been recorded at a slower tempo and the tape may have been sped up just a bit. If that's true, it may be of some consolation when you first try to get this groove up to speed. Notice that the feel is in-between straight and swung, but closer to the straight side of the spectrum. The "open" hi-hats happen almost accidentally, as Clyde was most likely tapping eighth notes with the heel of his left (hi-hat) foot and lifting his whole foot off the pedal ever so slightly for the quasi-open notes. (This technique has also been used to great effect by Bernard Purdie.) Also, this should be played with a fairly light touch; the break sounds so big because of the reverb applied to this section of the tune.

I've heard Clyde say, **"If I would've known so many people were going to hear that thing, I would've played something hipper than that."**

Funny, Clyde, very funny.

JAMES BROWN

28. *"Funky Drummer"* **beginning groove, 1969, drums: Clyde Stubblefield, c. 98 bpm.**

*Clyde plays lots of variations and eventually morphs this into the break.
Here is the main groove.*

29. *"Funky Drummer"* **break at 5:32 in the original ("tambourine mix") of the tune.**

30. *"Funky Drummer"* **fade out at 9:10.**

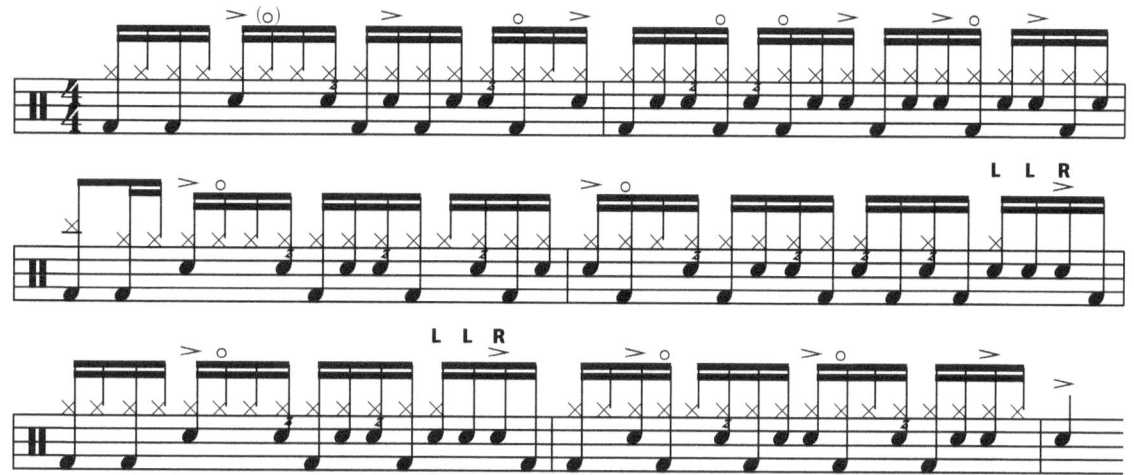

JAMES BROWN

PRACTICE TIPS FOR THE FUNKY DRUMMER

I've been working on the groove to "Funky Drummer" off and on for 15 years, easy. The hard part is getting the right hand up to speed and then getting everything else to fall into place. So... a couple of things I recommend. Check out the JoJo Mayer DVD *Secret Weapons for the Modern Drummer*. There's a section where he explains the push-pull technique for playing quicker continuous sixteenth notes in the right hand. Few humans will ever be able to do it the way JoJo does, but I found that just by practicing this technique a little bit, it helped get my right-hand sixteenths up to speed a little better.

Another tip is to practice the groove over and over at a slower tempo. You can use any number of software programs (such as Roni Music's Amazing Slow Downer, Seventh String's Transcribe!, Apple's Logic, or DigiDesign's Pro Tools) to slow down the track without changing the pitch. These programs usually have a function to loop it up as well. This allows you to hear exactly how Clyde is phrasing the sixteenth notes. You'll notice they are pretty straight, except that the snare drum skip beats and the note right before the backbeat on beat 4 are just a little swung. It's almost as if the right-hand (hi-hat) notes are straight and the left-hand (snare drum) notes are swung ever so slightly. You can really hear this when you slow it down. Practice the groove at a slower tempo so you can completely lock everything in. Get used to feeling where everything sits, and get used to the feeling of having it totally locked. You can practice to a metronome, but also practice to the slowed-down loop. Once you get it totally locked at the slower tempo, you can gradually increase the tempo to get it up to speed. Once you get it up to speed, try practicing it even a little quicker. This will make playing it at the right tempo a little easier as well.

As for the semi-shoops on the hi-hat, I tap my left heel in eighth notes on the hi-hat heel plate. When it's time for the "shoop," you just release the pressure with the ball of your foot ever so slightly... not really lifting up the foot, but just barely.

Also it helps to use a cranked metal snare drum and play it really lightly to get the sound. As far as I know, Clyde was using a 5x14 chrome-over-aluminum Ludwig Supra-Phonic 400. Clyde played lighter in the studio than most people realize.

You can apply these techniques to any other grooves you practice as well.

Mutiny!

1970 was a landmark year of turmoil and innovation in the James Brown camp. Most of the legendary '60s band, including Maceo Parker, Fred Wesley, Bernard Odum, and Jimmy Nolen, were disgruntled with pay and touring conditions and approached James before a March 9 concert in Columbus, Georgia. James was unwilling to meet the band's demands and immediately sent his Learjet to Cincinnati to pick up a band of teenagers, led by Bootsy Collins and his brother Phelps ("Catfish"). Brown knew of the Collins brothers because his record label, King, was also located in Cincinnati. The brothers and their crew were fans of Brown and knew most of the material, but the transition was not perfectly smooth and it took a few weeks for the new band to get up to speed. While the old band had featured a large horn section and multiple guitarists and drummers, the new band (named the J.B.'s) was more focused around the stripped-down rhythm section of one bass player (Bootsy Collins), one guitarist (Catfish Collins), and drummer Jabo Starks (who stuck around because he felt he had a contract to honor).

Once James felt the J.B.'s were ready for the studio, he took them in on April 25 to record "Get Up (I Feel Like Being A) Sex Machine." The tune was a monster hit, and James Brown and his band were back on track once more.

JAMES BROWN

31. "Get Up (I Feel Like Being A) Sex Machine" 1970, drums: John "Jabo" Starks, c. 109 bpm.

Note how much swing Jabo is putting on this groove.

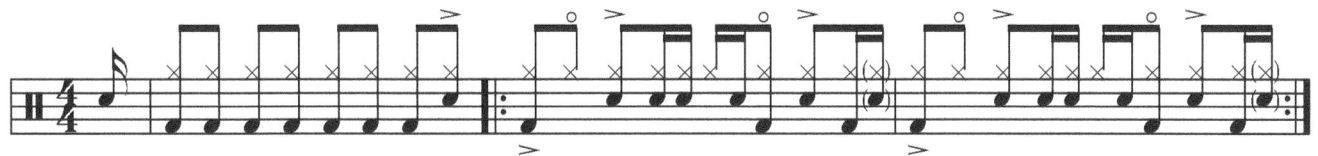

After the success of "Sex Machine" with his new monster band, James wasted no time getting back in the studio to crank out some more hits.

Here's Jabo's groove to "Super Bad." Again, notice the similarities to "Big Chief." The "3" side of the clave is heavily accented here.

32. "Super Bad" 1970, drums: John "Jabo" Starks, c. 127 bpm.

And here's the bridge. Notice the similarities in the right hand to the jazz ride cymbal pattern.

33. "Super Bad" bridge: First 8 bars.

JAMES BROWN

It's interesting to note that while Clyde Stubblefield was not part of the mutiny, he only appeared on a few tracks during this period. Here's a look at Clyde's groove to "Since You've Been Gone." Notice the missing 1: Very rare. Also, notice the similarity of beat 1 in this groove to beat 3 in the second bar of Nat Kendrick's "Soul Food."

34. "Since You've Been Gone" 1970, drums: Clyde Stubblefield, c. 116 bpm.

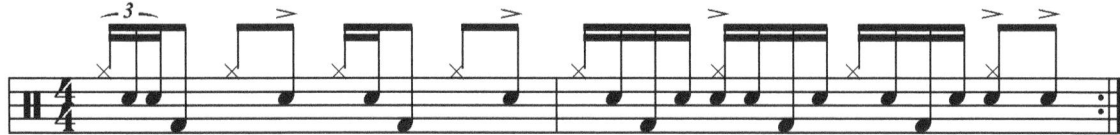

And here is Clyde's driving groove on the kick-ass remake of "Give It Up Or Turnit A Loose," recorded in 1970 as well. The drum and conga breakdown in this tune is another frequently sampled groove.

35. "Give It Up Or Turnit A Loose" break at 5:13, 1970, drums: Clyde Stubblefield, c. 117 bpm.

Here is Jabo's groove to "Talkin' Loud And Sayin' Nothing." The four-on-the-floor bass drum pattern makes this groove relentless.

36. "Talkin' Loud And Sayin' Nothing" 1970, drums: John "Jabo" Starks, c. 102 bpm.

Let's check out "Get Up, Get Into It And Get Involved." This track, along with the previous two Clyde grooves, are rare tracks where Clyde and Bootsy Collins appear together. Talk about a monster rhythm section!

37. "Get Up, Get Into It And Get Involved" 1970, drums: Clyde Stubblefield, c. 111 bpm.

JAMES BROWN

Here's Jabo's super slinky groove to "Soul Power." Notice the similarities to "Sex Machine."

38. "Soul Power, Parts 1 & 2" 1971, drums: John "Jabo" Starks, c. 104 bpm.
This one is played more in-between straight and swing.

Just one year and 16 days after they joined the James Brown camp, Bootsy and crew moved on and eventually hooked up with George Clinton's Parliament Funkadelic. For more about this important time in James Brown's legacy, check out the record *Funk Power* and it's liner notes.

With Clyde in and out of the band after 1970, Jabo began to play on a lot more hits and actually went on to play on more hits than any other James Brown drummer. Let's check out some more of Jabo's grooves. Notice the similarities to "Sex Machine" in some of the following examples. Although the grooves are similar, Jabo puts a unique spin on each of them. Make sure to listen and play along to each.

39. "Make It Funky" 1971, drums: John "Jabo" Starks, c. 96 bpm.

40. "Pass The Peas" 1971, drums: John "Jabo" Starks, c. 98 bpm.

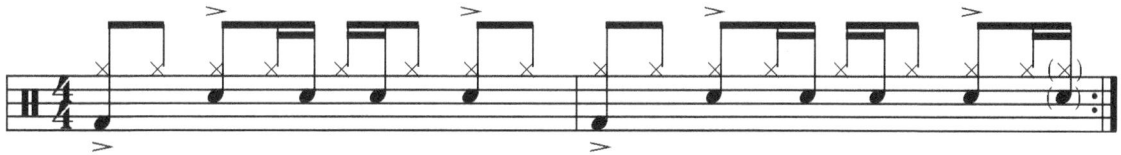

41. "I Know You Got Soul" Bobby Byrd 1972, drums: John "Jabo" Starks, c. 113 bpm.
Notice that this one is phrased more towards straight than swing.

42. "Stoned To The Bone" 1973, drums: John "Jabo" Starks, c. 100 bpm.

JAMES BROWN

43. *"Papa Don't Take No Mess"* **1974, drums: John "Jabo" Starks, c. 97 bpm.**

This is the basic groove, although Jabo improvises and varies the groove throughout.

Now let's further examine some of Clyde's classic grooves.

44. *"The Chicken"* **Alfred "Pee Wee" Ellis 1968, drums: Clyde Stubblefield, c. 96 bpm.**

45. *"Think (About It)"* **Lyn Collins 1972, drums: Clyde Stubblefield, c. 112 bpm.**

This one has a standout break that has been sampled to great effect.

46. *"Think (About It)"* **break.**

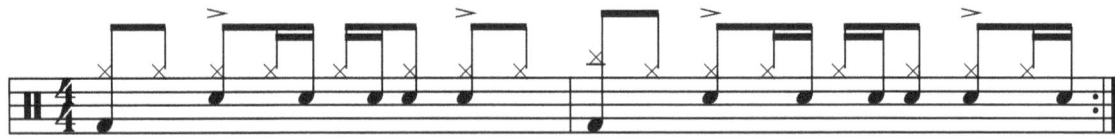

47. *"Hot Pants-I'm Coming"* **Bobby Byrd 1972, drums: Clyde Stubblefield, c. 112 bpm.**

JAMES BROWN

48. "Make It Good To Yourself" 1973, drums: Clyde Stubblefield, c. 117 bpm.

Finally, I'd like to summarize some of the differences and nuances of Jabo's and Clyde's styles. While these are generalizations, they tend to be true in most cases.

Also, make sure to check out Jabo and Clyde's joint DVD *Soul of the Funky Drummers* to see these funk masters demonstrate their styles firsthand.

Jabo

- *Tended to play more on the swing side of the spectrum*
- *Played lighter and more laid-back in general*
- *Played skip beats on the hi-hat*
- *Hi-hat pattern was often similar to the jazz ride cymbal pattern*
- *Often played one-bar phrases (which made his beats relentless)*
- *Sparse, light bass drum*
- *Often played ghost notes that required some jazz independence*

Clyde

- *Tended to play more on the straight side of the spectrum*
- *Played heavier and more aggressively in general*
- *Played straight hi-hat*
- *Hi-hat pattern was quarters, eighths, or sixteenths*
- *Often played two-bar phrases (but because he phrased his sixteenth straighter, his beats were relentless as well)*
- *Heavier, more active bass drum*
- *Often played chatter notes after or before the backbeat, or both*

GROOVE ALCHEMY

ZIGABOO MODELISTE

UNDERSTANDING ZIGABOO MODELISTE

It's no surprise that Joseph "Zigaboo" Modeliste of New Orleans funk supergroup the Meters is one of my all-time favorite drummers. Zig is one of the all-time legends when it comes to funk and groove drumming. Many drumming greats such as Steve Jordan, Dennis Chambers, Dave Weckl, and Vinnie Colaiuta cite Zig as one of their favorites as well.

As much as Zig is revered, I find that his playing is often misunderstood and misinterpreted. Let's begin by examining Zig's amazingly funky groove to the Meters' classic "Cissy Strut." Also note that the melody of "Cissy Strut" has an underlying 3-2 clave.

Interestingly, this groove is very linear in nature which was slightly ahead of its time, as linear drumming didn't become popular until the mid '70s.

49. "Cissy Strut" first A section, The Meters 1969, drums: Zigaboo Modeliste, c. 88 bpm.

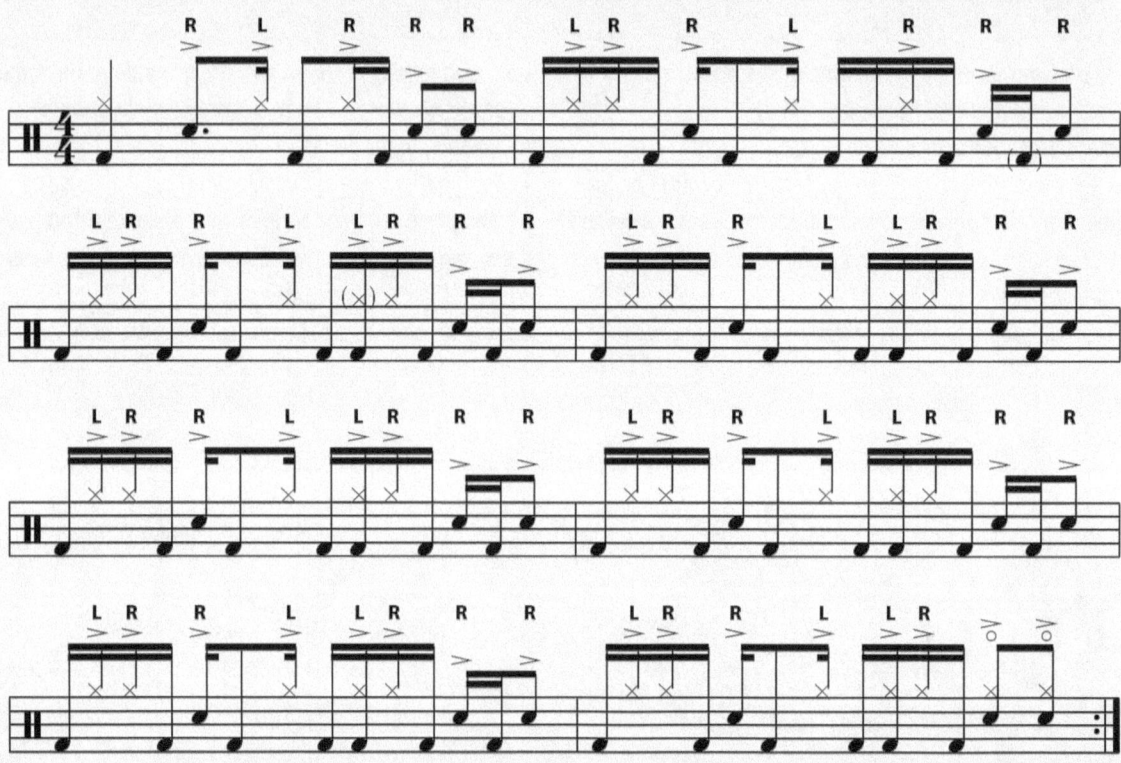

It is important to note that Zig played this beat with both hands on the hi-hat…gasp!!! I've seen many great drummers misinterpret this beat with just the right hand playing the hi-hat. I was fortunate to see Zig give a very rare clinic. He revealed that he used to watch a drummer by the name of Stanley Ratcliff (or "Rat") playing on Bourbon Street in the mid-'60s. Rat was the first drummer Zig saw play alternating sixteenth notes with both hands on the hi-hat. Zig thought this groove was incredibly funky…and rightfully so.

That groove looked like this.

50. "Ratcliff beat" c. 90 bpm.

ZIGABOO MODELISTE

Note that Zig played something very similar to this groove on "Groovy Lady."

51. "Groovy Lady" 1969, drums: Zigaboo Modeliste, c. 97 bpm.

Zig took this groove and started experimenting with it. He added some accents and syncopation and left some spaces, and voilà—the groove developed into Zig's beat for the A section of "Cissy Strut."

Let's try morphing the "Ratcliff beat" into "Cissy Strut."

52. AUDIO ONLY

To me, the "Ratcliff beat" is the key to unlocking a lot of Zig's other beats. Once you understand this beat and the fact that Zig was playing "Cissy Strut" with both hands on the hi-hat, a lot of Zig's other grooves start to make a lot more sense.

Now let's look at the groove to the B section of "Cissy Strut."

53. "Cissy Strut" First B section, *The Meters* 1969, drums: Zigaboo Modeliste, c. 88 bpm.

Do you see the similarities in this groove to the traditional New Orleans second line?

ZIGABOO MODELISTE

Now let's look at the beat to "Funky Miracle."

54. "Funky Miracle" *Look-Ka Py Py* 1970, drums: Zigaboo Modeliste, c. 96 bpm.

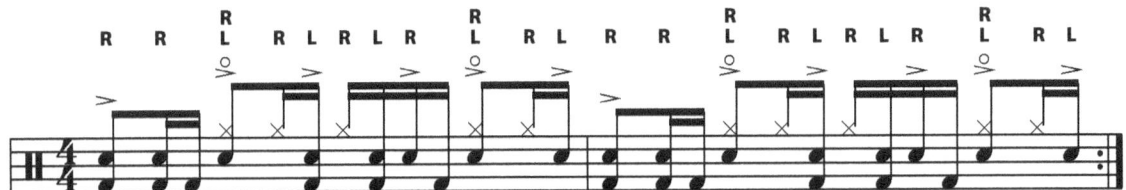

Note that this beat is very similar to "Cissy Strut," but the hands have been moved from the hi-hat to the snare, with the right hand going back up to the open hi-hat for the backbeats. If you play "Cissy Strut" with the right hand on the hi-hat and then try to play "Funky Miracle," they seem like two unrelated grooves. But when you understand that "Cissy Strut" is played with both hands on the hi-hat, the similarities between the two become obvious.

Now let's check out the correlation between the "Ratcliff beat" and "Hey Pocky A-Way." If you take away the backbeat on the snare, slow the beat down slightly, and move both hands to the snare, you have "Hey Pocky A-Way."

55. "Ratcliff beat" morphing into "Hey Pocky A-Way." AUDIO ONLY

56. "Hey Pocky A-Way" *Rejuvenation* 1974, drums: Zigaboo Modeliste, c. 83 bpm.

Note that although this beat is in-between straight and swung, it leans more to the swing side of the spectrum.

Now let's look at "Jungle Man."

57. "Jungle Man" *Rejuvenation* 1974, drums: Zigaboo Modeliste, c. 90 bpm.

And "Fire On The Bayou."

58. "Fire On The Bayou" *Fire On The Bayou* 1975, drums: Zigaboo Modeliste, c. 97 bpm.

ZIGABOO MODELISTE

You can see the correlation between the "Ratcliff beat" and some of these other Zig classics. My hope is that understanding this "key" will help unlock some of the mysteries of Zigaboo's style of playing.

Let's take a look at some of Zig's other grooves as well. Keep in mind that Zig varies things a good bit. I've notated the main grooves.

59. "Live Wire" *The Meters* 1969, drums: Zigaboo Modeliste, c. 115 bpm.

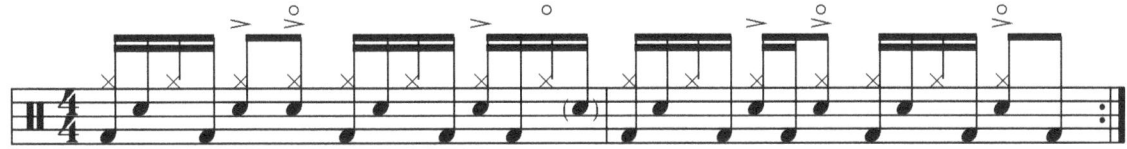

60. "Look-Ka Py Py" *Look-Ka Py Py* 1970, drums: Zigaboo Modeliste, c. 88 bpm.

Note that this groove is basically Zig's interpretation of the first bar of Clyde Stubblefield's groove to "Cold Sweat."

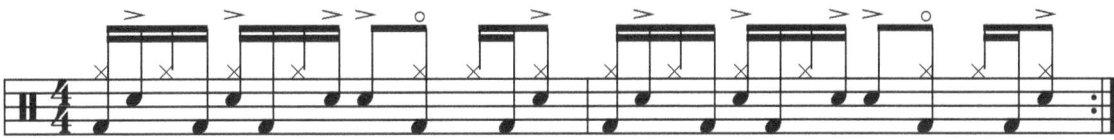

61. "Look-Ka Py Py" break at 00:49.

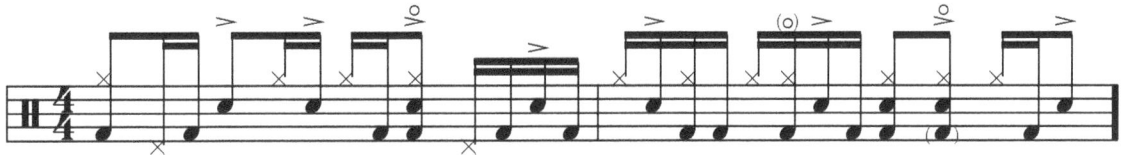

62. "Pungee" *Look-Ka Py Py* 1970, drums: Zigaboo Modeliste, c. 80 bpm.

Notice that Zig doesn't play any cymbals other than the hi-hat throughout this tune.

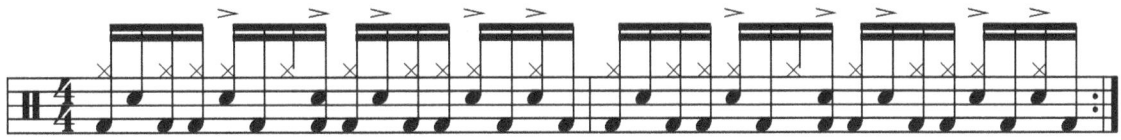

63. "Little Old Money Maker" *Look-Ka Py Py* 1970, drums: Zigaboo Modeliste, c. 103 bpm.

A SECTION *First 4 bars:*

ZIGABOO MODELISTE

64. B SECTION

Here's the four-bar break in "Oh, Calcutta!" This break occurs at 1:41 in the tune. Bars 1 and 2 were sampled for the Amerie hit "1 Thing" (2005).

65. "Oh, Calcutta!" break at 1:41, *Look-Ka Py Py* 1970, drums: Zigaboo Modeliste, c. 104 bpm.

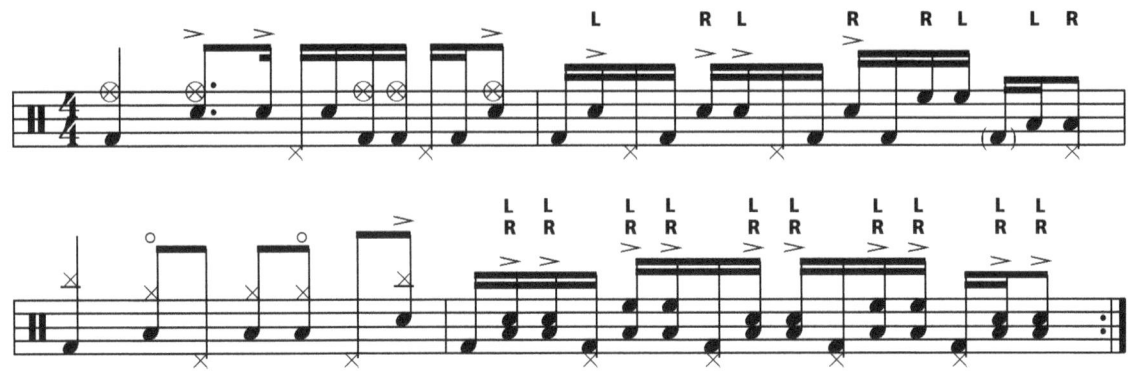

66. "Tippi-Toes" *Struttin'* 1970, drums: Zigaboo Modeliste, c. 90 bpm.

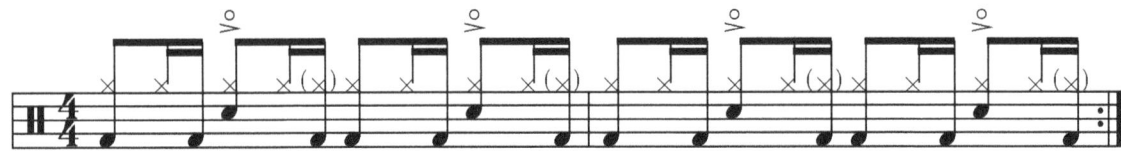

67. "Hey! Last Minute" two-bar intro, *Struttin'* 1970, drums: Zigaboo Modeliste, c. 93 bpm.

Zig's groove is based off the first bar of the intro. Notice the similarities to "Cissy Strut."

ZIGABOO MODELISTE

68. *"Hey! Last Minute"* **break at 1:17.**

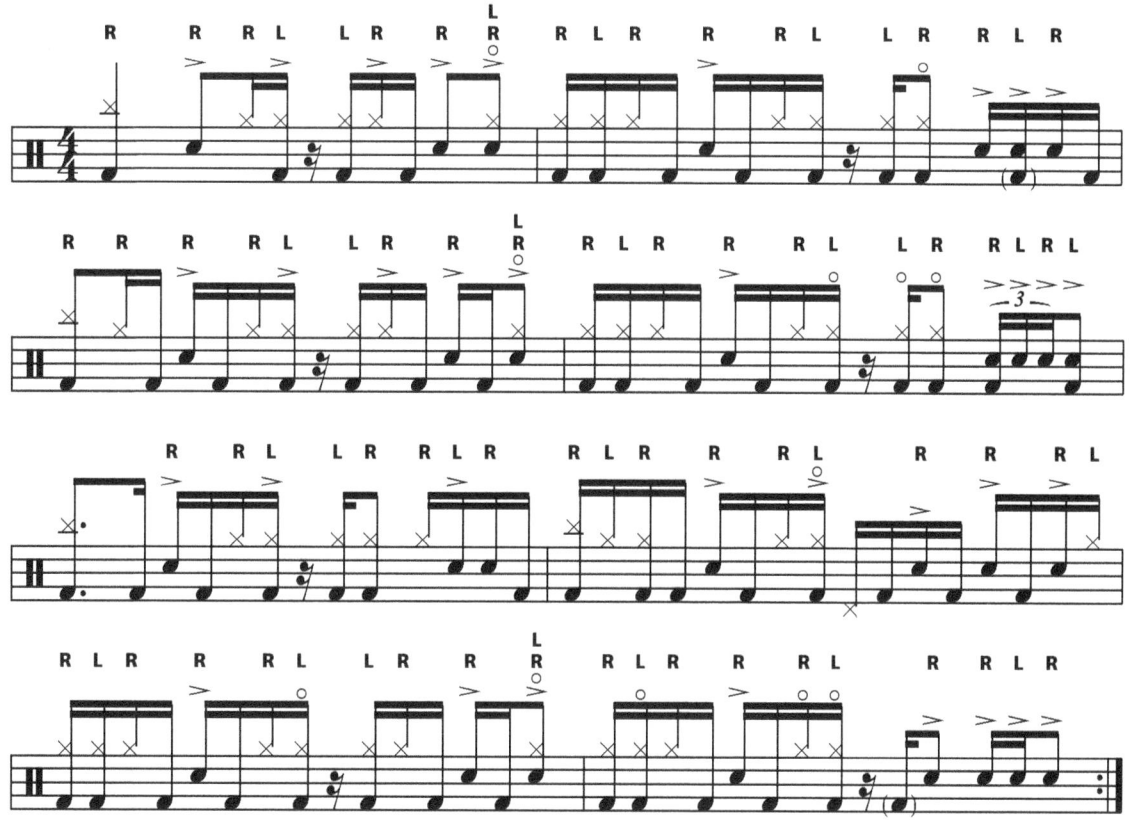

69. *"People Say"* *Rejuvenation* **1974, drums: Zigaboo Modeliste, c. 103 bpm.**

70. *"Just Kissed My Baby"* *Rejuvenation* **1974, drums: Zigaboo Modeliste, c. 85 bpm.**

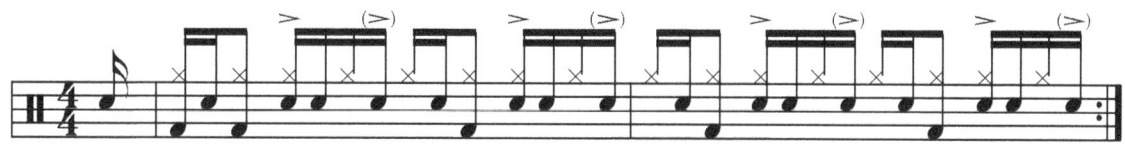

71. *"Africa"* *Rejuvenation* **1974, drums: Zigaboo Modeliste, c. 95 bpm.**

ZIGABOO MODELISTE

72. "Africa" *Live On The Queen Mary* 1975, drums: Zigaboo Modeliste, c. 94 bpm.

Zigaboo Modeliste

PLAYING IN-BETWEEN THE CRACKS

I think now is a good time to talk about the concept of playing "in-between the cracks." A lot of the preceding beats from Zigaboo, Clyde Stubblefield, and Jabo Starks will groove much better if you have a deeper understanding of this concept.

I've spoken previously in *Take It To The Street* (DVD, Carl Fischer) about playing in-between the cracks, or playing with a feel that is in-between straight and swing. Now let's look at how to apply this feel to funk and other types of grooves. Phrasing in this way can make your playing feel more organic and less mechanical. Many of the great groove players that have stood out over time grew up listening to music that swung. Earl Palmer, John Bonham, Bernard Purdie, Zigaboo Modeliste, Idris Muhammad, Clyde Stubblefield, and Jabo Starks all grew up hearing Big Band, swing, jazz, be-bop, blues, jump blues, rhythm and blues, and early rock 'n' roll. All of this was music that swung. So, when drummers eventually started playing straighter in rock 'n' roll and funk settings, a natural lope was present in their playing. Now that we have all grown up and lived through a period of time where things have been quantized and straightened out to the nth degree, we have to readdress how to achieve this lope in our playing. I think it is important to understand this way of playing in order to deepen your pocket. It is also helpful to have this feel in your arsenal should your playing situation call for it.

There are several things we can work on to develop this. First let's play hand-to-hand (RLRL-RLRL) sixteenth notes on the hi-hat with a backbeat on 2 and 4. Start off playing straight sixteenth notes, then gradually morph towards swing. You want to feel all the areas between straight and swing. Live in the middle for a while and try to internalize the way this feels. Once you feel comfortable there, move towards the swing end of the spectrum. You can even move past swing, all the way to flams. Once you're ready, move back through the spectrum, stopping in the in-between area for a while, then continue morphing all the way back to straight.

It's important to do this with a metronome so that you don't move the time, just the phrasing. Also note that the right hand will be playing straight eighth notes while the left hand is doing the morphing.

Start off with this groove.

This illustration may help you visualize what you are trying to accomplish.

PLAYING IN-BETWEEN THE CRACKS

Once you're comfortable with that exercise, let's re-examine the "Ratcliff beat." Try doing the same thing with this beat. Again, this groove is the key to understanding a lot of what Zigaboo Modeliste does. Getting the right feel on this is imperative if you want to understand Zig's approach.

74. "Ratcliff beat" morphing from straight to swing, c. 90 bpm.

Once you've experimented with morphing this beat, try locking it into Zig's phrasing on the Meters' "Groovy Lady" (ex. 51).

Again, if you move the hands to the snare and accent the bass drum notes instead of the backbeat, the "Ratcliff beat" becomes "Hey Pocky A-Way." Getting this feel down will help you understand where Zig and a lot of the New Orleans stuff is coming from. You can practice a lot of the stickings from *Take It To The Street* to "Hey Pocky A-Way" as well. It's important to remember that this groove is slightly more swung than "Cissy Strut" or "Groovy Lady," but it is still in-between straight and swing. Let's try morphing "Hey Pocky A-Way." Let's start in-between where it should be, then listen to how wrong it sounds as it morphs towards too straight and then too swung. Once you get comfortable playing it in-between, try practicing to the original version of the tune.

75. c. 83 bpm .

You can apply this concept to right-hand sixteenth notes on the hi-hat as well. Try morphing the following groove with the right hand on the hi-hat.

76. c. 90 bpm

Once you feel comfortable with that, try this one as well.

77. c. 90 bpm

PLAYING IN-BETWEEN THE CRACKS

James Gadson's drumming is another great example of this style. He has a great way of phrasing right-handed sixteenth notes in-between straight and swing. Notice that Gadson tends to lean toward the straight end of the spectrum.

Let's check out some of Gadson's killer sixteenth-note grooves.

78. "Express Yourself" Charles Wright and the Watts 103 St. Rhythm Band 1970, drums: James Gadson, c. 92 bpm.

79. "Ain't No Sunshine" Bill Withers 1971, drums: Al Jackson Jr., c. 80 bpm.

Although James Gadson played on many Bill Withers tracks, this one was actually played by Al Jackson Jr. Here's what he plays on the vamp-out of the tune starting at 1:38.

80. "Use Me" Bill Withers 1972, drums: James Gadson, c. 77 bpm.

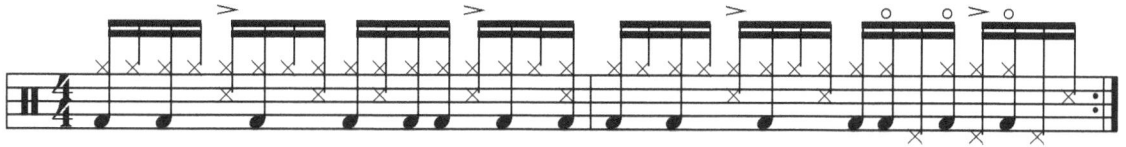

81. "Kissin' My Love" Bill Withers 1972, drums: James Gadson, c. 92 bpm.

First 4 bars:

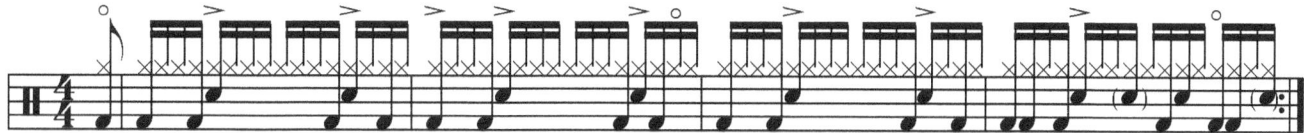

Once you feel comfortable playing in-between straight and swing, try applying this concept to the grooves in this book, as well as any other grooves in your vocabulary.

I've noticed a natural tendency when initially trying to apply this feel is to swing the notes too much. I've found that it's better to err on the side of straight. It tends to make things more funky. Just make sure not to straighten it out too much. The key is to listen to the masters of this style and continue to adjust and refine your feel to fit the music you are playing. Also remember to record yourself playing this way and compare it to past and present masters of this concept.

GETTING CREATIVE
AND APPLYING THE "ATIONS"

In this section we'll examine some of the creative processes involved in groove-based and funk drumming. We've examined some of the techniques that should be digested and what has come before. Now I'd like to explore how we can combine some of these different aspects to create new grooves and come up with your own approach.

We can start by examining and understanding how some of our favorite drummers created their classic grooves. We will try to develop a deeper understanding of some of the masters' creative processes. We'll examine some of the building blocks and where they got some of the ideas to do what they did. We can then begin to create grooves of our own by using certain techniques that can aid in the creation process.

We can now begin to apply some creative techniques I like to call the "ations." These would include examination, variation, style and tone combination, new application, realization, exploration, improvisation, interpretation and inspiration. We can also experiment with feel and tone juxtaposition as well.

GROOVE ALCHEMY

GETTING CREATIVE

EXAMINATION AND VARIATION: CLYDE & JABO

Let's start off by further examining some of the details and nuances of Clyde and Jabo's styles. By developing a deeper understanding of where these guys were coming from, we can internalize some of the elements of their styles so we can apply these elements in new ways.

Let's check out some of the elements that comprise Clyde's groove to "I Got The Feelin'." Clyde plays lots of variations throughout the tune, so I've transcribed the first 26 bars here.

82. "I Got The Feelin'" 1968, drums: Clyde Stubblefield, c. 128 bpm.

continued on next page

GETTING CREATIVE

GETTING CREATIVE

As we take a closer look at this groove, we notice that Clyde took elements of some of the James Brown drummers who came before him and added in some of his own flavor to create something new. The displaced backbeats were originally pioneered by James Brown himself in 1962 (on the tune "Limbo Jimbo") and further developed by Nat Kendrick and Clayton Fillyau in 1963 (on "Soul Food, Parts 1 & 2" and "Signed, Sealed and Delivered," respectively). The open hi-hat on the & of beats 1 and 3 was borrowed from Melvin Parker. Clyde then added a bit of himself with his chatter notes. As we've noted before, some of these chatter note phrases are made up of three sixteenth notes in a row and have a backbeat or accent in the middle of the three notes.

So, we can see that Clyde "borrowed" a couple of elements from the drummers before him, combined them, and then added an element of himself to come up with something new.

James Brown, Nat Kendrick, Clayton Fillyau + Melvin Parker + Clyde Stubblefield =
"I Got The Feelin'"

Now, after digesting this and some of Clyde's grooves from earlier, we can try to come up with variations based on his ideas. These are grooves that, to the best of my knowledge, Clyde himself hasn't recorded. After getting comfortable with these, try to come up with some variations of your own.

83. c. 112 - 130 bpm

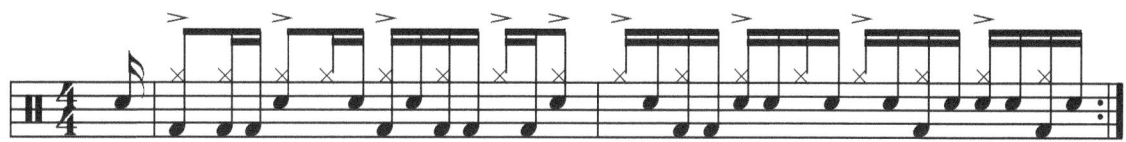

84.

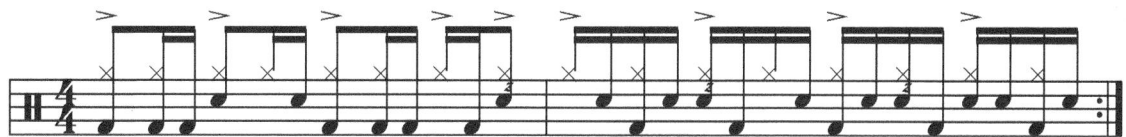

85.

86.

GETTING CREATIVE

87.

88.

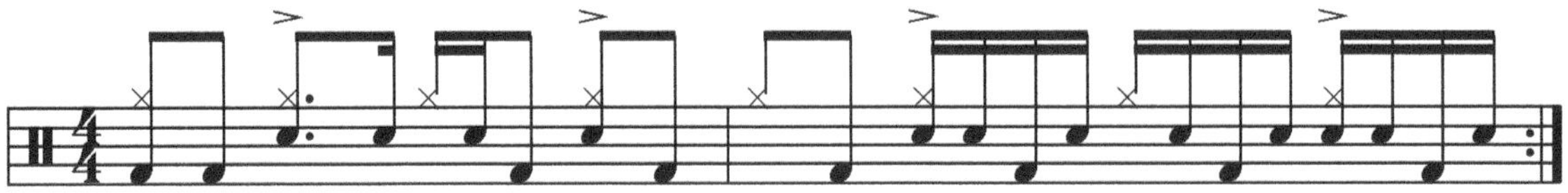

89.

90.

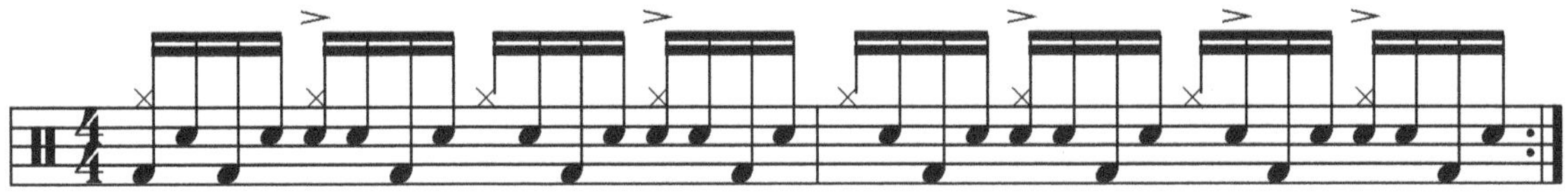

91.

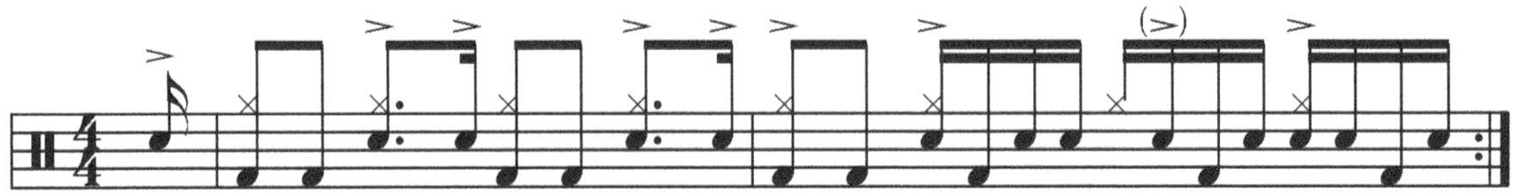

92.

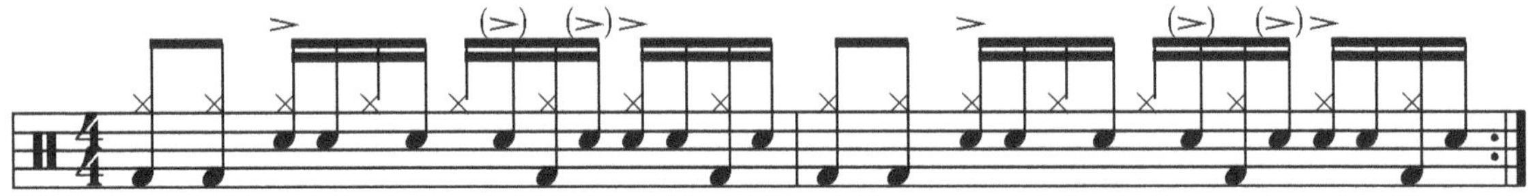

93.

94.

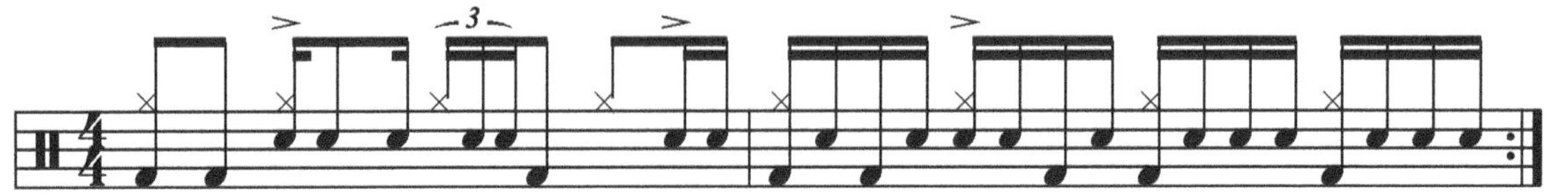

GETTING CREATIVE

Here's one that even hints at Jabo's groove to "Sex Machine."

95. c. 109 bpm

Here are some "Funky Drummer" variations.

96. c. 98 bpm

97.

98.

If you need to increase the tempo and play these at a slightly quicker pace, it helps to leave some notes out. Here are some variations with strategic spaces that can help make these grooves more feasible to play at quicker tempos.

99. c. 105 bpm

100.

GETTING CREATIVE

101.

102.

103.

104.

105.

106.

107.

108.

GETTING CREATIVE

You could also adapt "Funky Drummer" to higher tempos by using this common sticking: RLRR-LRRL.

109. c. 120 - 170 bpm

And this one varies that sticking in order to get back Clyde's grace note before the second backbeat.

110. c. 120 bpm

111. c. 110 bpm

Now let's further examine some of Jabo Starks' playing. Let's start by taking a closer look at Jabo's groove to "Sex Machine." This groove is very representative of Jabo's playing with James Brown.

Note: In examples 112-133, the sixteenth notes are swung.

112. "Get Up (I Feel Like Being A) Sex Machine" 1970, drums: John "Jabo" Starks, c. 109 bpm.

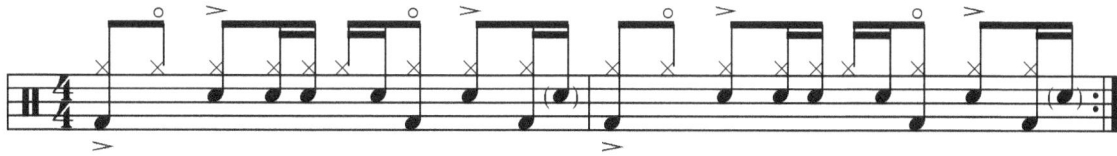

As we look more closely at this groove, we can see that at its foundation it is basically a slowed-down version of Clayton Fillyau's groove to "I've Got Money." Jabo also borrowed the open hi-hat on the upbeats of 1 and 3 from Melvin Parker. Coming from a strong jazz background, Jabo added skip beats on the hi-hat and swung his sixteenth notes a good deal. Check out how similar Jabo's hi-hat pattern is to the jazz ride cymbal pattern. Jabo was basically playing jazz with a backbeat.

In jazz, the term "tippin'" refers to swinging hard with a very light touch up on top played with the very tip of the stick on the cymbal. Try to think of this while playing these Jabo ideas.

113.

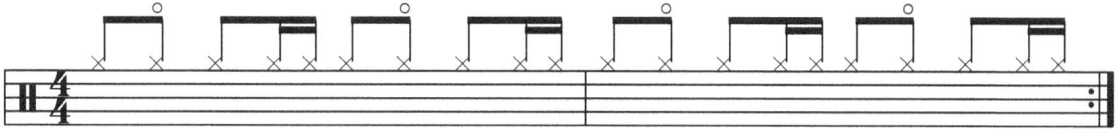

GETTING CREATIVE

114.

115.

116.

Clayton Fillyau + Melvin Paker + Jabo Starks = "Sex Machine"

It's interesting to note that different people have different interpretations of how this beat was played. I've seen it notated this way…

117.

And this way.

118.

Jabo plays this simplified version on the bridge of the album version.

119.

GETTING CREATIVE

You can even hear Jabo play these variations on some of the live versions.

120.

121.

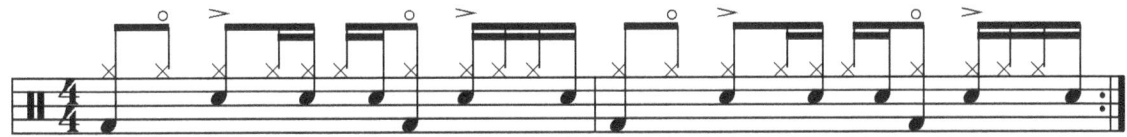

122.

123.

124.

125.

126.

GROOVE ALCHEMY

GETTING CREATIVE

127.

128.

I actually got to have dinner with Jabo and Clyde. After hanging out and getting to know each other a bit, I said to Jabo, "I really didn't want to do this to you, but since you're right here, let me ask you. I've heard and seen your grooves interpreted a bunch of different ways. I think you're doing this, and it's coming from the jazz ride cymbal pattern." Then I played this on his leg…

129.

He smiled and said, "That's it! Very few people understand that, but that's right."

I think it's important to realize that Jabo himself played many variations on the original recordings and played things slightly different live as well. It's important to check out all of these variations and use the ones that fit the situation at hand.

Let's check out some variations on Jabo's grooves.

130.

131.

GETTING CREATIVE

132.

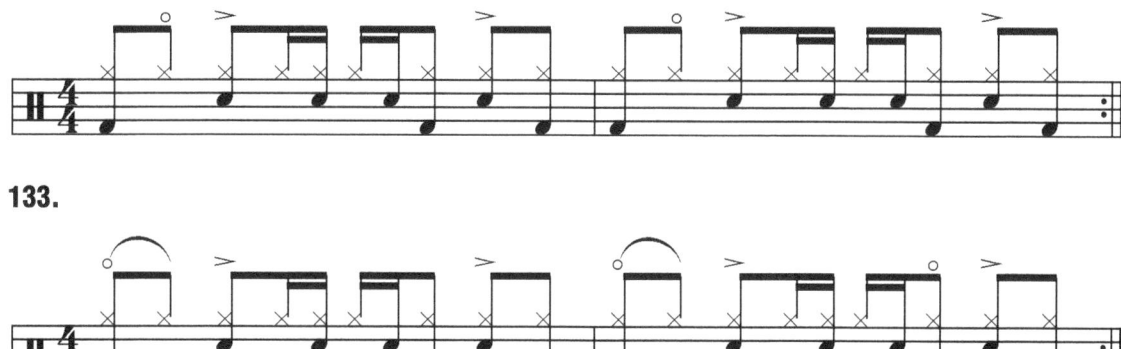

133.

Varying Zigaboo

Let's start with a four-bar thing I came up with to explore some of the possibilities of the accents and space Zig was experimenting with in his groove to "Cissy Strut."

Zig Exploration

We can take Zig's hi-hat ideas and stretch them over the bar line.

134.

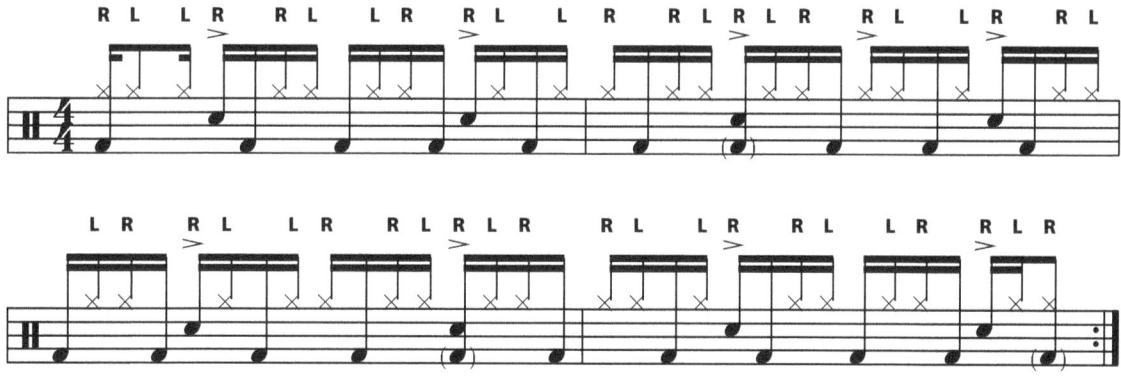

Now let's create some grooves from the discoveries we've just made.

135.

136.

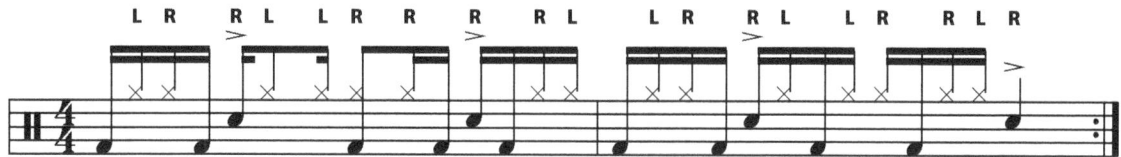

GROOVE ALCHEMY

GETTING CREATIVE

137.

138.

An effective variation tactic can be to rearrange a pre-existing groove or start it in a different place. You can then add variations from there. Check out how this next groove is based off of ideas found in "Cissy Strut" and "Hey! Last Minute." This new groove starts out with what were beats 3 and 4 of those grooves.

139.

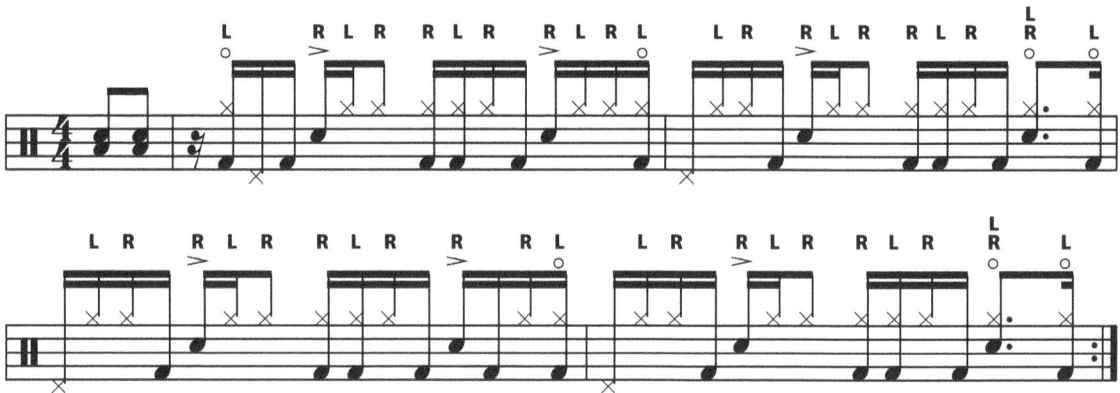

Now let's see how this new groove works in a tune.

140. "Pie-Eyed Manc" **FULL MIX**

Here are some variations on the groove to the live version of "Africa."

141.

142.

GETTING CREATIVE

Here are some variations on "Fire On The Bayou" that integrate the LLRL-RLRR sticking. These would work for "Slippin' Into Darkness" or any type of Bo Diddley context as well.

143.

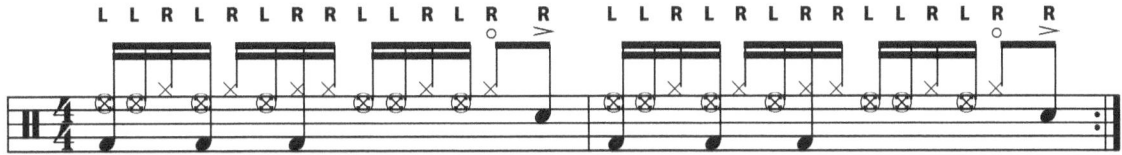

144.

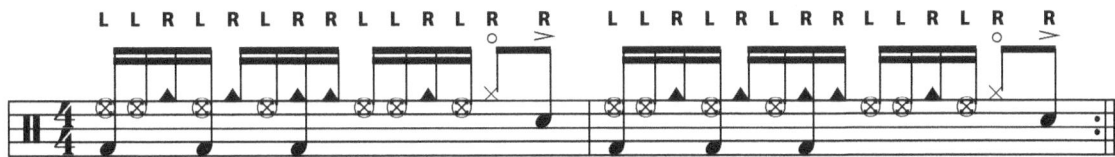

145.

146.

147.

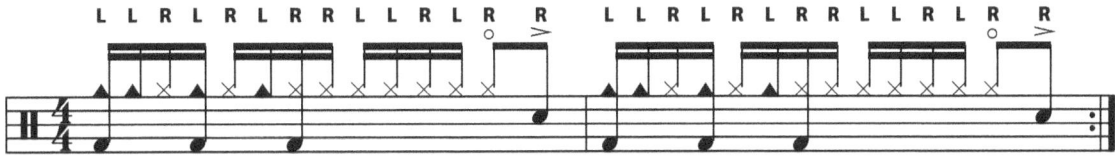

You can even get "Fire On The Bayou" variations with the RRLR-RLRL sticking.

148.

GETTING CREATIVE

149.

I've talked previously in *Take It To The Street* about how you can get "Hey Pocky A-Way" variations with the Steve Gadd Mozambique. The right hand conveniently plays the tambourine pattern in the "Hey Pocky A-Way" drums and percussion breakdown. These sound great with a tambourine or ching ring on the hi-hat.

150.

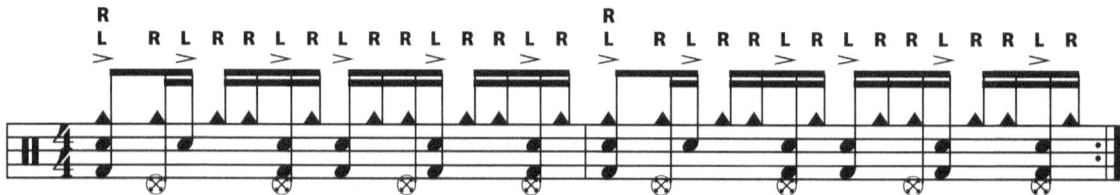

Try a handbourine or jingle stick in the right hand as well.

151.

Experiment with moving the right hand around to different voices on the kit. Here's one with the handbourine on the cowbell and the hi-hat/tambourine playing with the bass drum.

152.

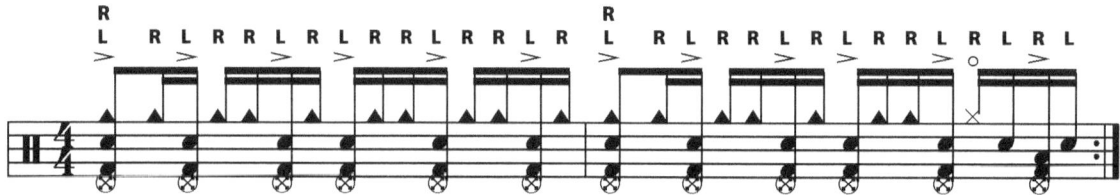

Hopefully, examining these grooves and variations ignites some creativity and you are able to come up with some new variations of your own. Experiment with these grooves, variations, and creative processes and try to come up with some new grooves that have never existed before.

GETTING CREATIVE

STYLE COMBINATION

Now that we've examined and varied some of these classic grooves, let's try to come up with some new grooves by combining the styles of some of the masters. Let's start by combining Jabo and Clyde. These next few grooves are two-bar grooves. The first bar is based off of Jabo's one-bar groove to "Sex Machine," and the second bar is comprised of variations inspired by what Clyde plays in "I Got The Feelin'." Clyde tends to play a bit straighter than Jabo, so you may want to experiment with splitting the difference in-between straight and swung.

153.

154.

155.

156.

157.

158.

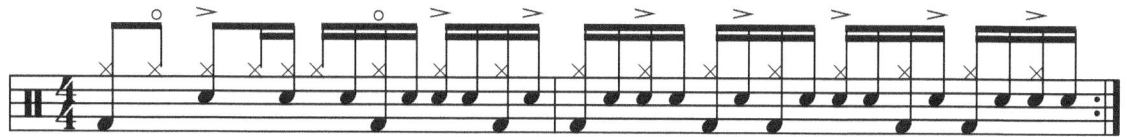

GETTING CREATIVE

159.

160.

161.

Now let's put some of these ideas into a song.

162. *"Pot Licker"* **FULL MIX**

GETTING CREATIVE

Here are a few that incorporate Clyde's chatter notes into Jabo's groove to "Sex Machine."

163. c. 110 bpm

164.

165.

166.

Here are some that continue in that vein, but start to get away from "Sex Machine."

167.

168.

169.

GETTING CREATIVE

170.

171.

172.

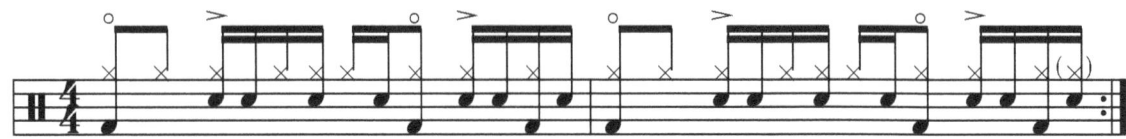

Here are a few that use Jabo's groove to "Super Bad" as the first bar while still drawing from Clyde for the second bar.

173. c. 125 bpm

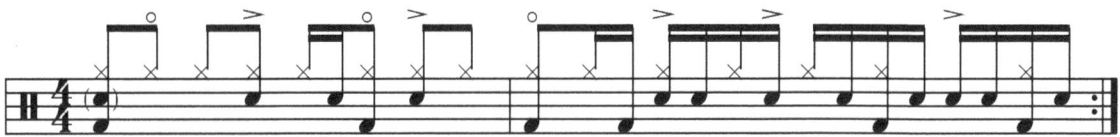

174.

175.

GETTING CREATIVE

176.

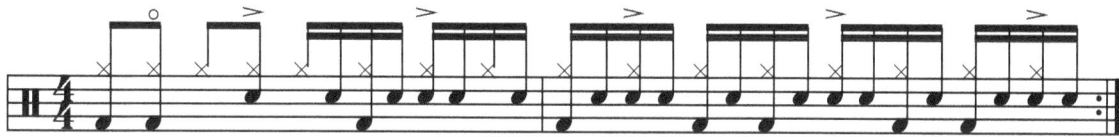

177.

Once you get comfortable with some of these, try experimenting on your own to come up with new takes on combining ideas from these two great players.

This concept of combining Jabo and Clyde is not entirely new. Check out this groove that Steve Jordan draws from often. Notice that he uses Clyde's approach to chatter notes but tends to swing the notes more, á la Jabo. Also notice that Steve brings the right hand down to the snare drum for a strong backbeat on beat 4 in the first example.

178.

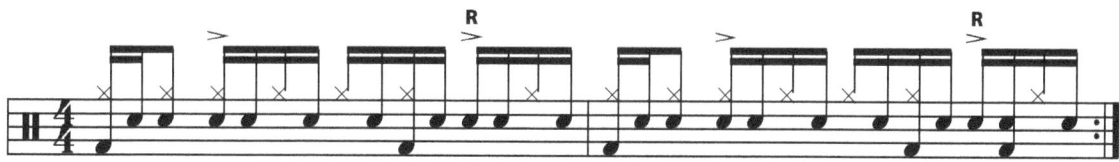

179.

180.

181.

GETTING CREATIVE

Sometimes, seemingly different styles can be mixed with some of these ideas to create a new twist. Let's try infusing some of Stewart Copeland's drumming into some of these ideas. Stewart often uses accents on his ride cymbal or hi-hat to great effect. He also improvised and varied what he played greatly. Let's apply a Stewart Copeland-esque rhythmic structure on the hi-hat and/or bell of the ride.

182.

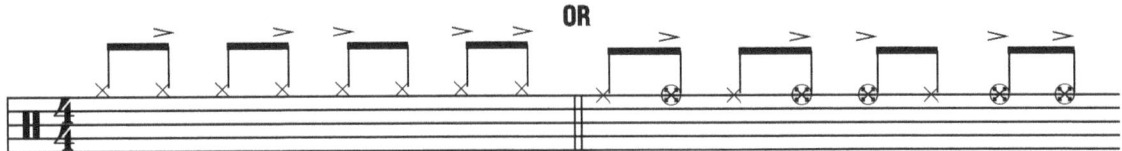

Note that a similar accent structure appears in some hip-hop and funk drumming. It even appears in John Bonham's groove to "When the Levee Breaks." These "accents" happen when compression is applied to the drums. Compression makes the softer notes louder and the louder notes softer, and gives the drums more crunch and more punch. When compression is applied to simple beats and the hi-hat is the only note being played at that time, it tends to jump in volume and sound like an accent.

If we apply this accent structure to these types of grooves, we start to come up with some very interesting, forward-moving grooves. You can hear some of these ideas in the previous tune, "Pot Licker" as well.

183.

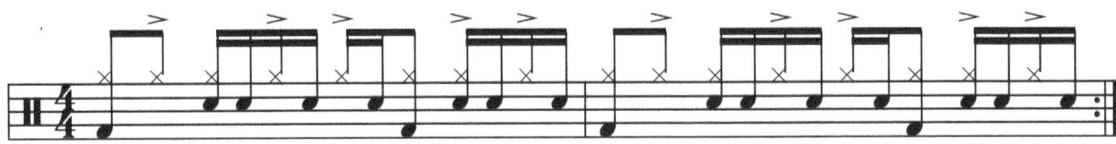

184.

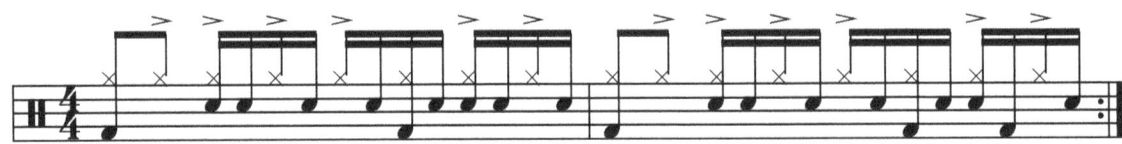

185.

186.

GROOVE ALCHEMY

GETTING CREATIVE

We can further develop this idea and continue to push the envelope with what I call "Power Clyde" grooves. Some of these start to get away from the Stewart Copeland-esque ride pattern.

187.

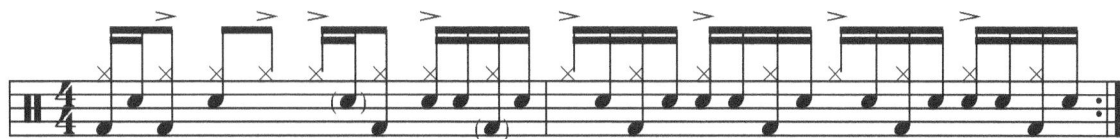

188.

189.

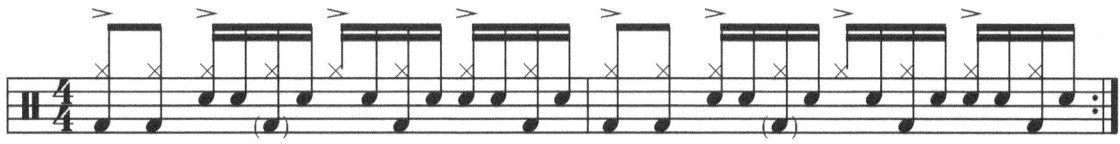

190.

Now we can start to incorporate some upbeat sixteenth notes in the right foot. This really starts to drive things. John Bonham used this idea to great effect.

191.

GETTING CREATIVE

Once the right foot starts doing upbeat sixteenth notes, you can also add upbeat eighth notes with the left-foot bass drum to add to the overall drive. I do this more to assimilate some of the things "Geechie" from the Wild Magnolia Mardi Gras Indians does on a bass drum with mallets rather than playing traditional "double bass." Geechie usually plays a bass drum resting on a hotel luggage stand so that the head is facing up. He plays it with a bass drum mallet in the right hand and the back end of a bass drum mallet in the left hand with traditional grip. The rhythms he plays are usually based off of the cinquillo rhythm ♪♪♪ ; ♪♪ or variations thereof. He plays the rhythms with his right hand and fills in with the left. The stickings created will look familiar and usually look like this: RLRR-LRRL-RLRR-LRRL or RLRR-LRRL-RRLR-RLRL. Sometimes Geechie will sit on the RRLR-RLRL sticking as well. This creates an awesome rolling, rumbling feeling when played in conjunction with a kit drummer or other percussionists.

I often use a 26-inch bass drum that is played with a remote pedal just to the right of my main pedal. So for me, the upbeat sixteenth notes are on the 26 while the upbeat eighth notes are on the 20 (or 18). With the two different bass drums I try to approximate the rumbling, rolling, percolating effect that Geechie gets with what he plays. When I do this, I like to straddle the hi-hat at the same time. This sounds great if you add a tambourine or ching ring on top of the hi-hat as well. With this setup, it sounds better if the left-foot bass drum is softer than the right.

192.

We can start to mix some of these "Power Clyde" concepts with the beat for "Big Chief" and come up with some very compelling grooves.

193.

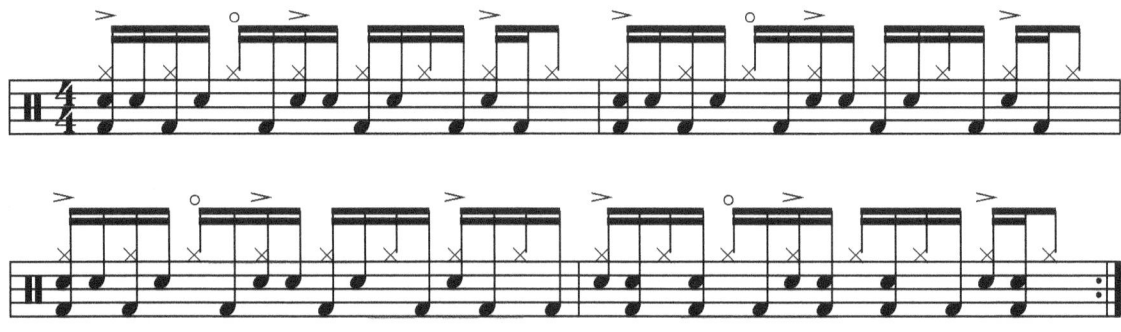

194.

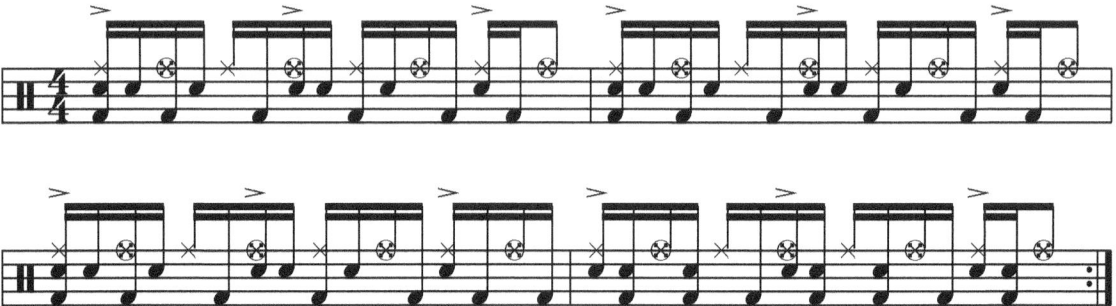

GETTING CREATIVE

195.

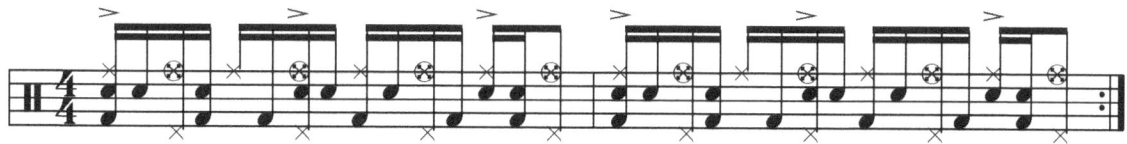

Here's one that is a slightly sparser Clyde/"Big Chief" variation.

196.

As before, you can add upbeat eighth notes on the left-foot bass drum and hi-hat. By playing this variation of the mambo bass drum pattern with the right foot and the upbeat eighth notes with the left, you can get the cinquillo rhythm in the bass drums.

197.

You can also start incorporating upbeat sixteenth-note variations on the right foot.

198.

Then bring the left foot over to the bass drum and hi-hat and move the right to the 26".

199.

GROOVE ALCHEMY

GETTING CREATIVE

Now let's incorporate the two-bass-drum cinquillo and upbeat sixteenth-note patterns into one massive, rolling, Clyde Stubblefield-inspired Power "Big Chief" groove!

200.

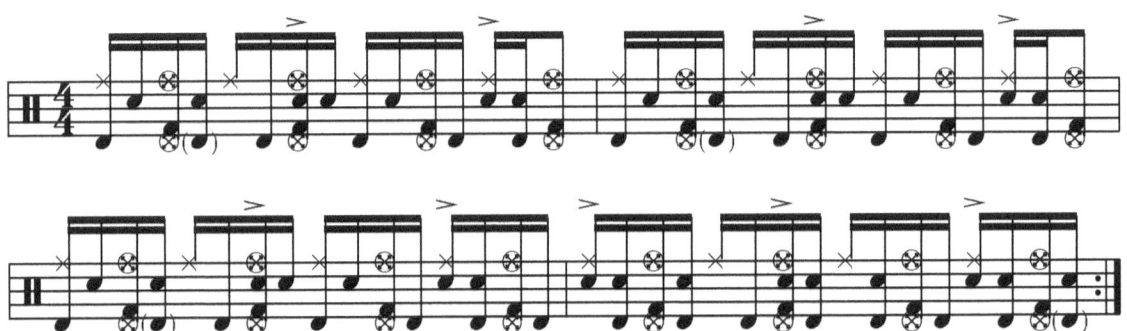

FEEL AND TONE JUXTAPOSITION

Now we can try a creative technique I like to call "feel juxtaposition." This concept entails infusing a pre-existing groove with a different feel to come up with something new. You can change the tempo, or change the feel of something to force you to look at it in a different light.

Consider the way the drum breaks to the Winstons' "Amen Brother" and James Brown's "Soul Pride" were sped up to create a new genre…drum & bass.

I personally like to slow things down and put a New Orleans lilt to it. Let's re-examine example 153, which is a combination of Jabo's groove to "Sex Machine" and Clyde's groove to "I Got The Feelin'." Imagine what this groove (these notes) would sound like slowed down a bit and played by Zigaboo Modeliste. Keep in mind that Zibaboo doesn't usually play ghost notes as dramatically as Jabo and Clyde.

201. Similar to 153 but juxtaposing a New Orleans (or Zigaboo) feel on to it.

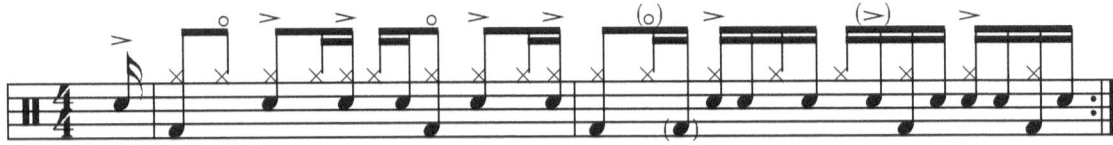

Let's revisit the groove to the previous song. This time it has a different feel.

202. *"Pot Licker… Slight Return"* **FULL MIX**

Now let's try some tone juxtaposition. Move the right foot to the 26-inch bass drum, switch out the snare drum, and imagine the same groove as played by John Bonham. Hopefully you can begin to see some of the possibilities for creating new things to play.

203. AUDIO ONLY Same notation as 201, but juxtaposed with Bonham-esque tones.

GETTING CREATIVE

Let's continue by utilizing a combination of styles and feel juxtaposition. Let's try mixing Zig with Clyde. Here are a few more variations. Play these with a "New Orleans lilt" that is in-between straight and swing, á la Zigaboo.

204.

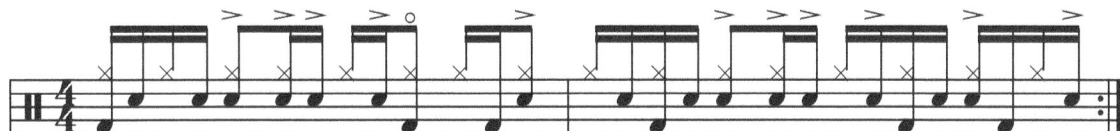

205.

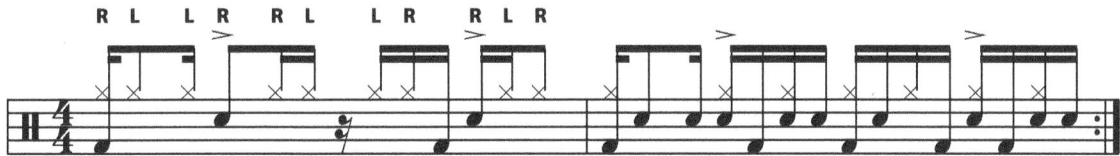

206.

207.

208. Let's take some of the Zig-inspired rhythmic ideas we were playing with both hands on the hi-hat and move them to the bell of the ride with the right hand.

209.

GETTING CREATIVE

210.

211.

212.

Now let's move the right foot to the 26-inch bass drum and put the John Bonham snare up again. Try playing any of the previous examples this way.

213. AUDIO ONLY Similar to 211, but played differently.

Let's try mixing Clyde with John Bonham. Imagine this groove played to "Immigrant Song" on Bonham's drums.

214.

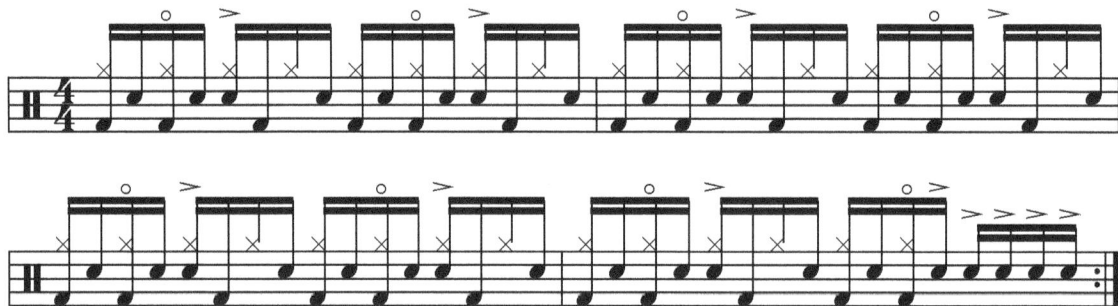

GETTING CREATIVE

215.

3x

216.

3x

Now let's check out David Garibaldi's groove to "Soul Vaccination." Here's the groove the way it was originally played.

217. *"Soul Vaccination"* ***Tower of Power*** **1973, drums: David Garibaldi, c. 106 bpm.**

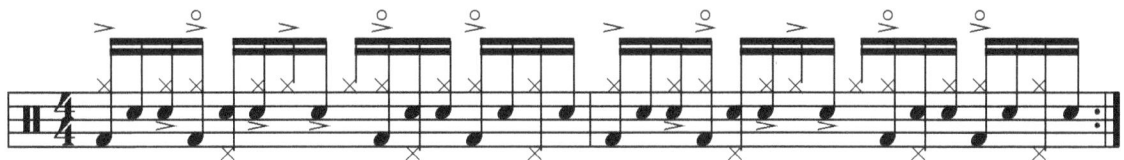

At first glance, this type of groove may seem to be completely removed from some of the New Orleans funk grooves. But if you take this groove, slow it down to 88 bpm, and apply the "New Orleans lilt," you get a syncopated, modern-sounding New Orleans groove. Check out how this sounds on the track.

218. AUDIO ONLY Same notation as 217, but played differently.

Note that David Garibaldi based a lot of his grooves on Swiss triplets. He experimented with the accents and bass drum placement to come up with interesting beats that fit the songs and style of Tower of Power. Also notice that in this groove David incorporates the RLRR-LRRL-RRLR-RLRL sticking. David first became aware of the RLRR-LRRL sticking from a tune called "Prehistoric Rhythm (And The King Kong Beat)" by the band Redbone.

As you improvise with this concept while maintaining an in-between straight and swung feel, you can come up with more grooves in this domain.

Check out these variations.

219.

GETTING CREATIVE

220.

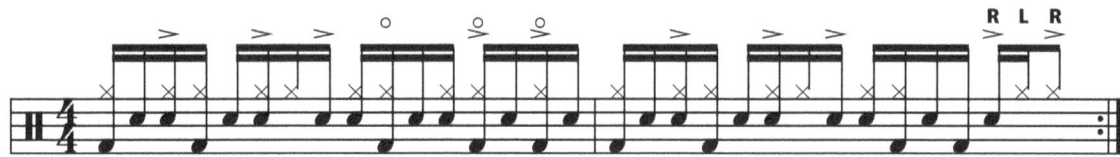

221.

You can add some buzzes for variation as well.

222.

Here's one that goes to the bell of the ride.

223.

You can change the accents slightly and start to hint at the traditional New Orleans street beat accents.

224.

Now you can take this and put the right hand on the cowbell or move the right hand to other parts of the kit to continue to come up with new grooves.

225.

GETTING CREATIVE

Here are a few that start to get away from the original "Soul Vaccination" but are still rooted in the same idea.

226.

227.

228.

229.

Here are a few that work well in a modernized New Orleans context.

230.

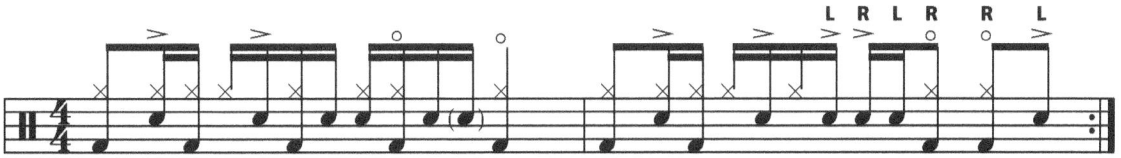

231.

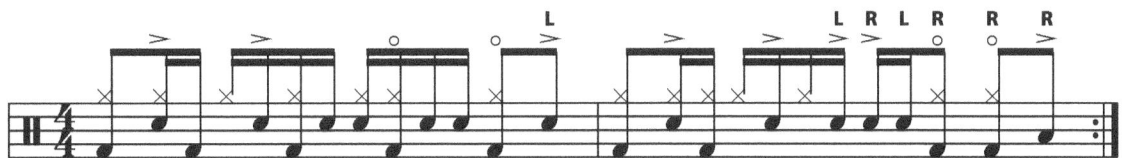

GETTING CREATIVE

Now let's apply some of these grooves to a tune.

232. *"Root Cellar"* FULL MIX

Let's further explore some of the possibilities you can achieve with Swiss triplets. Note how the accents change. The first two are over the mambo bass drum pattern. The second two utilize the concept of having the bass drum chase the accents. These are designed to help free you up physically so you can execute any ideas you may come up with while improvising in this vein.

233. Swiss triplet explorations.

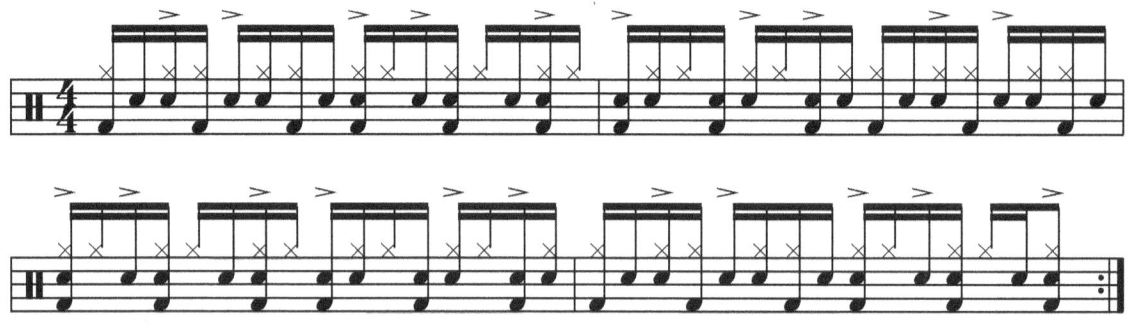

234.

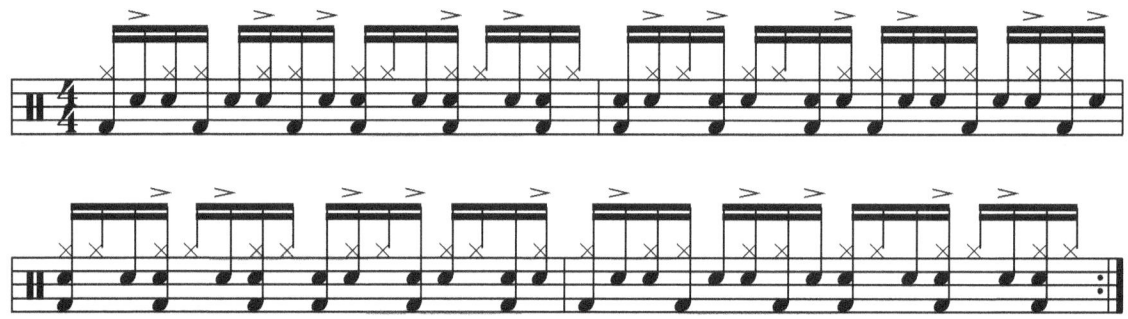

235.

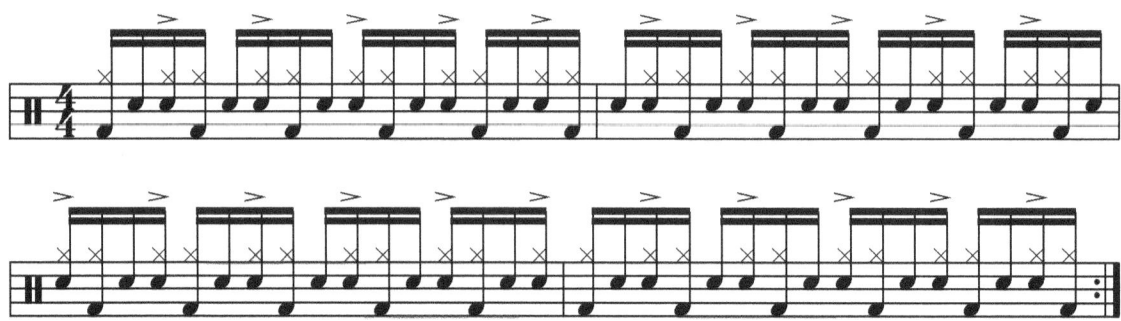

GETTING CREATIVE

236.

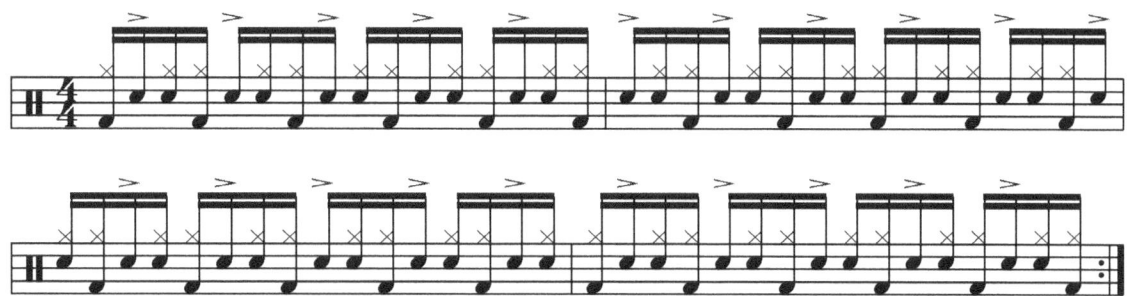

You can improvise with these concepts in mind and come up with many variations. Check out the following improvisation based on this concept...

237.

Now...when I do this I try to step outside of myself, watch what I'm doing, and remember any good ideas. Let's check out what happens if we pick out the good bars and loop them up, or just play them repetitively...

238. Looped from bars 1 and 2 of example 237.

239. Looped from bars 6 and 7 of example 237. You can then experiment with tempo, texture and tone and hopefully come up with some new ideas.

GETTING CREATIVE

Now let's take a look at some examples of Mike Clark's playing.

Here's a transcription of the first 16 bars of Mike's playing on the tune "Actual Proof."

Notice some familiar influences creeping in here. There's Clyde's chatter notes, the right hand "King Kong" pattern ♪♫ ; ♫ , the occasional missing "1," and creative placement of open hi-hat notes. Also note the subtle underlying 3-2 modified clave.

240. "Actual Proof" Herbie Hancock *Thrust* 1974, drums: Mike Clark, c. 123 bpm.

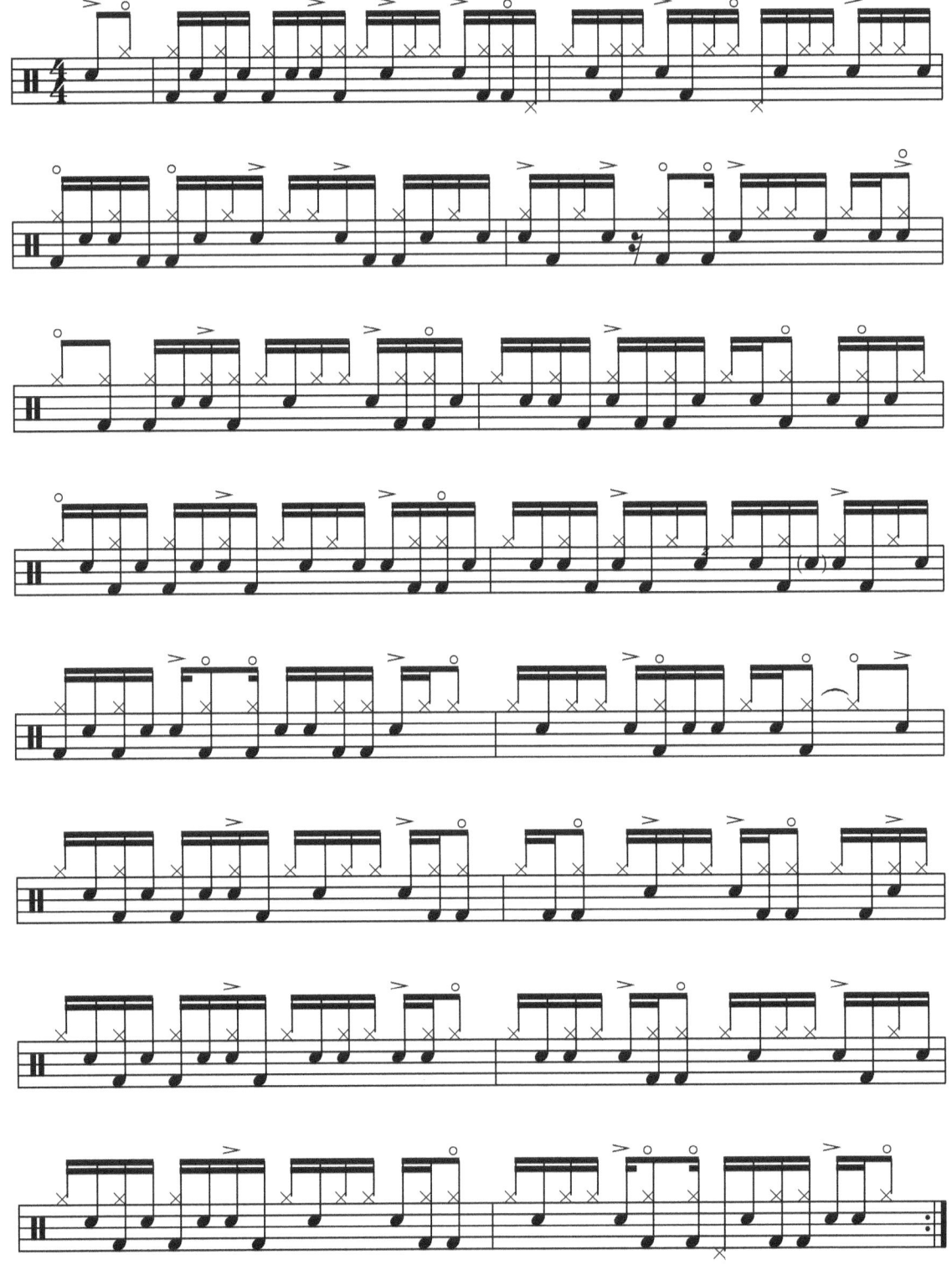

GETTING CREATIVE

If you see a lot of similarities in the playing of David Garibaldi and Mike Clark, that's because they both came up in Oakland, California around the same time and were influenced by a lot of the same music, namely James Brown with Clyde Stubblefield and the King Kong beat as played by Pete DePoe in the band Redbone.

Now let's try some variations on these concepts. This one is an "Actual Proof," "Big Chief" combination. You can play these in the upper tempo ranges à la Mike Clark, but I tend to use these in a slightly reduced tempo range and usually play them in-between straight and swung. I will demonstrate them that way here.

241.

Note both the fast modified 3-2 clave and the slow 3 clave exist at the same time with these.

242.

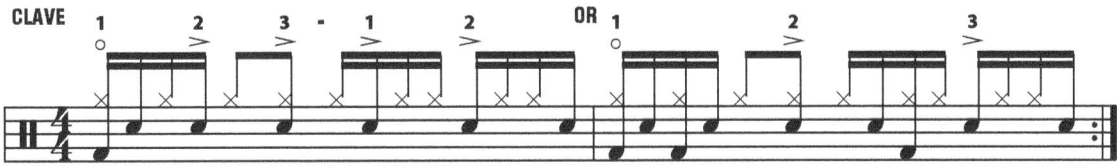

243.

244.

245.

246.

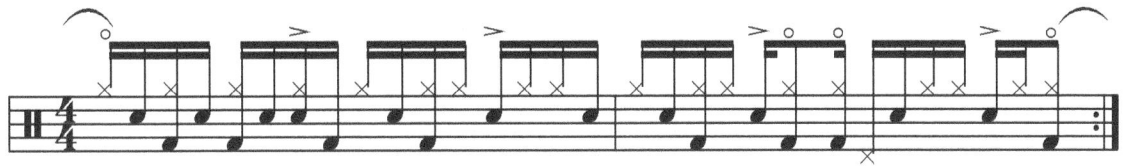

GETTING CREATIVE

247.

After you get comfortable, try varying and improvising on these beats. Try combining Garibaldi and Clark with each other and with other drummers. Try applying feel juxtaposition as well. Also try placing the hands on other sound sources within the kit. You'll be surprised and pleased with what you come up with. David Garibaldi's book *Future Sounds*, Mike Clark's book *Funk Drumming*, and Jim Payne's book *Give The Drummers Some!* (re-issued as *The Great Drummers of R&B, Funk & Soul*) are excellent sources for transcriptions of some of these grooves. You can also use these books as a deep well of great beats to reinterpret.

Interpretation

I've been talking a lot about learning things as they were originally played and then applying the "ations" to them. There can sometimes be a significant benefit to playing things wrong initially as well. You can always go back and learn something the "right" way, but you can't always re-harness the inspiration you feel the first time you hear something. Some times improvising over your first impression of something or playing your own interpretation of something can lead to new creative ideas that you may not have come up with if you had been locked in to learning something the "right" way or the way it was written in a book.

I've come up with lots of ideas by playing my interpretation of something I was excited about. Let's look at a specific example of this. As I was first learning the groove to "Cissy Strut," I didn't yet know that Zig had played it with both hands on the hi-hat and I was playing it with only the right hand on the hi hat. That looked something like this:

248.

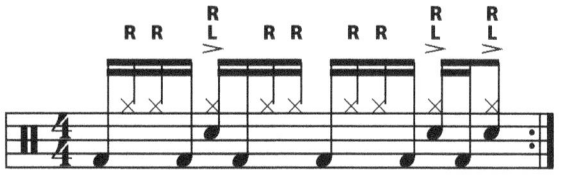

At the same time, I was also checking out some of David Garibaldi's grooves. I started to incorporate some Garibaldi-isms into my interpretation of "Cissy Strut"—namely swiss triplets. Below is a groove that is a combination of my interpretation of Zig and Garibaldi. If I had played "Cissy Strut" "correctly" from the start, I may never have come up with this groove.

I've written out the main groove. In the audio example I continue playing and move my hands to different voices around the kit while keeping the same groove happening. I've played this groove where I've played the hands on empty glass bottles. I used this for the tune "Stanton Hits The Bottle" on my first record, *All Kooked Out*.

249.

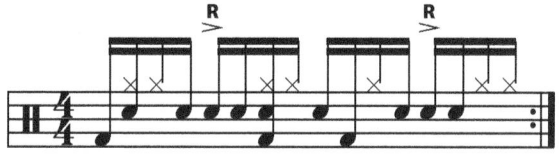

You can try playing your interpretation of any grooves that you hear. Try this with some of your favorite grooves and with any of the grooves with in this book. You may be surprised with what you come up with.

Don't be afraid of initial mis-interpretation or reinterpretation as well. When used in the right context, they can often lead to great ideas.

HI-HAT VARIATIONS

ONE OR TWO HANDS ON THE HI-HAT?

I usually consider there to be two approaches to funk drumming: either one hand on the hi-hat or both hands on the hi-hat. The first would be where one hand plays the hi-hat while the other hand plays the snare. Most commonly the right would play the hi-hat while the left plays the snare. This would change in the case of a left-handed or open-handed drummer. This approach was used very effectively by the James Brown drummers, and by David Garibaldi and Mike Clark. The second approach would be where both the right hand and left hand are free to play on the hi-hat while either the right or left hand plays the snare. As we've seen, this second approach was used very effectively by Zigaboo Modeliste.

With the first approach, the right hand plays all the notes on the hi-hat while the left hand plays the backbeats, grace notes, and accents on the snare. The right hand can play eighth notes, sixteenths, or any combination thereof. Clyde Stubblefield, Jabo Starks, James Gadson, and Benard Purdie usually played in this manner. "Funky Drummer," "Sex Machine," "Kissing My Love," and "Rock Steady" (respectively) are all good examples of their playing in this style.

David Garibaldi and Mike Clark came along later and added more linear, syncopated, and modern elements to this style. "Soul Vaccination" and "Actual Proof" (respectively) are good examples of David and Mike's playing in this style.

The second approach evolved out of playing sixteenth notes with both hands on the hi-hat. This allows you to play 2 and 4 backbeats with your right hand. We've examined this approach earlier in the drumming of Zigaboo Modeliste and his development of the "Ratcliff beat." "Cissy Strut," "Jungle Man," and "Fire On The Bayou" are all excellent examples of this style of playing.

Here are some classic grooves that utilize this concept. I've listed these in chronological order.

250. "It Ain't My Fault" Smokey Johnson 1964, drums: Smokey Johnson, c. 87 bpm.

Note the similarities in this beat to the traditional New Orleans second line.

251. "Cissy Strut" The Meters 1969, drums: Zigaboo Modeliste, c. 88 bpm.

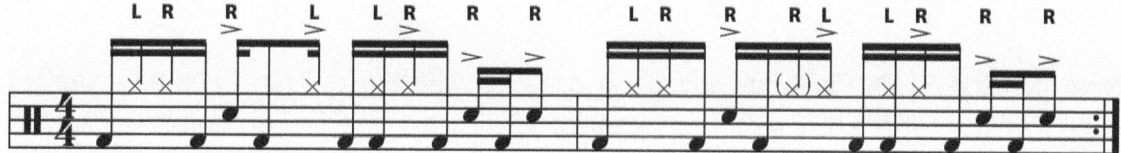

HI-HAT VARIATIONS

252. *"Slipping Into Darkness"* **War 1971, drums: Harold Brown, c. 88 bpm.**

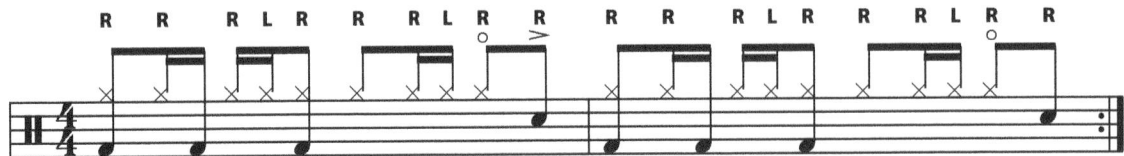

Notice the similarities to "Fire On The Bayou" (below). Harold was a big fan of New Orleans drummers. I'm sure he and Zig were checking out a lot of the same stuff as the basis for their own interpretations. Zigaboo was also a big influence on Harold Brown.

253. *"Jungle Man"* **The Meters 1974, drums: Zigaboo Modeliste, c. 90 bpm.**

Note the similarities to "It Ain't My Fault." Smokey Johnson was a big influence on Zig.

254. *"Fire On The Bayou"* **The Meters 1975, drums: Zigaboo Modeliste, c. 97 bpm.**

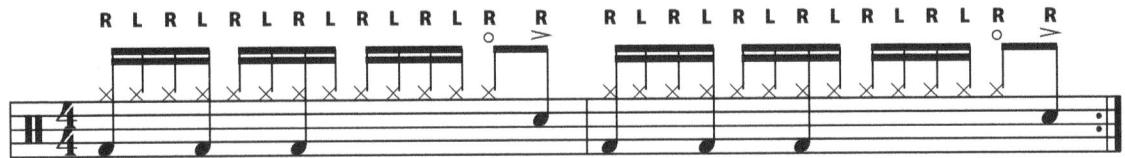

255. *"Tamborine"* **Prince 1985, c. 120 bpm.**

This groove has a lot of tambourine in the mix and it's hard to make out what was really played on the hi-hat. This is an approximation of the original groove.

Note that the RLRL-RLRL sticking stays constant with these. The rights play straight eighth notes while the lefts play the upbeat sixteenth notes. Subsequently if you leave out a downbeat or eighth note, you leave out the right. If you leave out a sixteenth note, you leave out the left. You could work on morphing any of these from straight to swing to find the magic area in-between, just as we did with the "Ratcliff groove" in the section "Playing In-Between the Cracks."

HI-HAT VARIATIONS

When improvising or trying to come up with new grooves, I like to combine the two approaches to come up with new ideas. The following are examples of some of the grooves I've come up with that combine right-hand lead and alternating hands on the hi-hat. Note that the right hand usually plays eighths and sometimes sixteenths, but the left is usually interjecting upbeat sixteenths. Interjecting the left like this makes the notes played by the left jump out dynamically and intensity-wise.

Note that stickings are marked when the left hand plays the hi-hat. If there is no sticking, play the hi-hat with the right hand and the snare with the left.

256.

257.

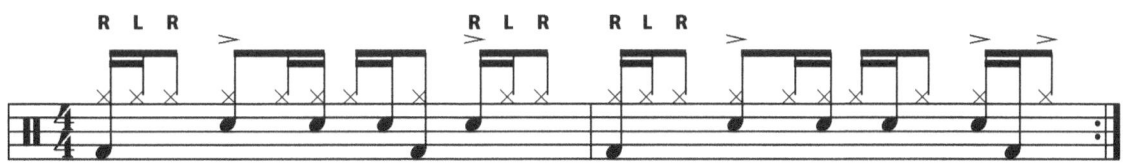

258.

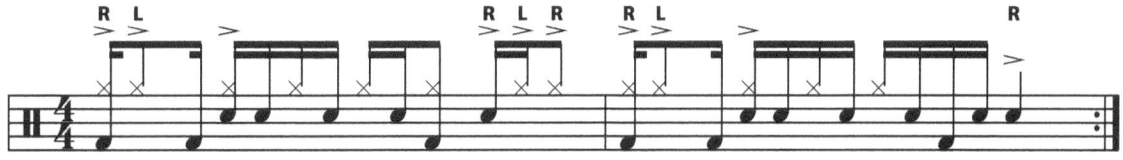

259.

260.

261.

HI-HAT VARIATIONS

And here's is one that combines Clyde, Jabo, and Zig.

262.

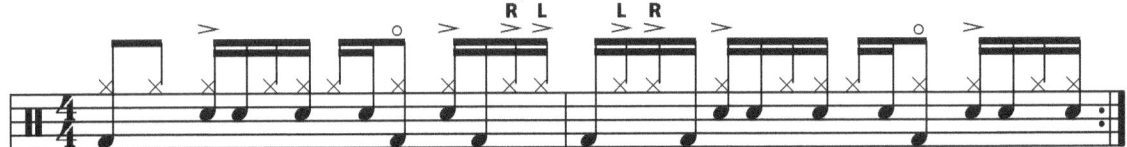

Once you get comfortable with the grooves here, try coming up with some of your own grooves utilizing this approach.

GROOVE ALCHEMY

CLAVE GROOVES/RHYTHMIC STRUCTURE

GROOVES WITH AN UNDERLYING CLAVE OR RHYTHMIC STRUCTURE

With most of the grooves I play, I like to lock into an underlying clave or rhythmic structure. The New Orleans second line is usually based off of a modified 2-3, 3-2, or 3-3 clave (the latter being where the groove sits on the 3 side of the clave). I've dealt extensively with 2-3, 3-2, and 3-3 clave grooves in my previous book *Take It To The Street*.

With jazz or swing, the pulse is the quarter note. With funk, the underlying structure is often bass drum on 1 with the snare on 2 and 4. But many other underlying rhythmic structures are possible. Take for instance Clyde Stubblefield's groove to the James Brown tune "Cold Sweat"…

263. "Cold Sweat" James Brown 1967, drums: Clyde Stubblefield, c. 112 bpm.

Let's now break this groove down to its underlying rhythmic structure.

264.

Now that we've stripped the original groove down to its basic rhythmic reference point, we can start to build up some variations on this rhythmic structure. This first one stays within the stylistic realm of Clyde Stubblefield.

265.

Here's one that adds in Jabo's jazz-influenced skip beats on the hi-hat. Play this one with and without the open hi-hats. Also try playing it on the ride.

266.

CLAVE GROOVES/RHYTHMIC STRUCTURE

Here are a couple with more of a jazz/boogaloo slant.

267.

268. This one hints at the style of Idris Muhammad.

269.

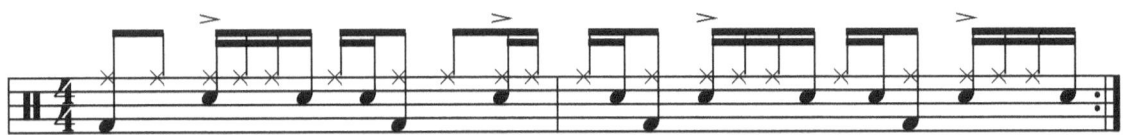

270.

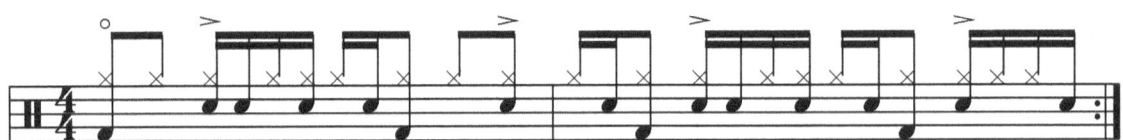

Here are a few that start to add some of the ideas I've derived from Zigaboo Modeliste.

271.

272.

273.

CLAVE GROOVES/RHYTHMIC STRUCTURE

274.

Now let's examine just the first bar of "Cold Sweat." John Bonham referenced the rhythmic structure of the first bar of "Cold Sweat" and reinterpreted it for his groove to the verses of Led Zeppelin's "Whole Lotta Love." Note that Bonham varied this groove from bar to bar, so this is an approximation.

275. "Whole Lotta Love" Led Zeppelin *Led Zeppelin II* 1969, drums: John Bonham, c. 93 bpm.

Here's a look at Bonham's reworking of the rhythmic structure.

276.

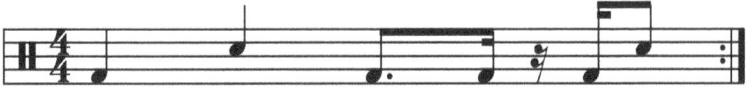

Zigaboo Modeliste also took the rhythmic structure of the first measure of "Cold Sweat" and did his own interpretation for the Meters' tune "Look-Ka Py Py."

277. "Look-Ka Py Py" The Meters *Look-Ka Py Py* 1970, drums: Zigaboo Modeliste, c. 88 bpm.

Here's a closer look at Zig's interpretation of the rhythmic structure.

278.

CLAVE GROOVES/RHYTHMIC STRUCTURE

Now let's string these two grooves together into a two-bar groove using Zigaboo-esque tones.

279.

Now let's reverse the order using John Bonham-esque tones.

280.

To me, John Bonham and Zigaboo Modeliste's styles are much more similar than they are different. Both drummers were born in 1948. The Meters' and Led Zeppelin's debut albums both came out in 1969. Both drummers grew up listening to Earl Palmer playing with Fats Domino and Little Richard, the drummers of James Brown (notably Clyde Stubblefield), Bernard Purdie, and Motown. Their individual playing is often different interpretations of the same or similar influences. Both drummers reinterpreted the first bar of "Cold Sweat" to create signature grooves of their own for the first tune on each of their second albums. They both played with a phrasing that was in-between straight and swing. The more you check out both of these masters, the more you will see they are really two sides of the same coin from opposite sides of the pond.

Let's check out some variations on this structure. Once you get comfortable with these, you can try reversing the order of the bars.

281. c. 91bpm with Zig-like tones.

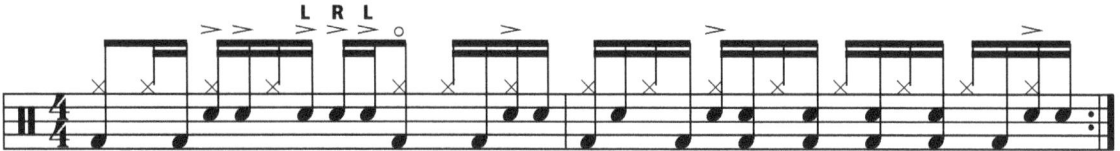

282.

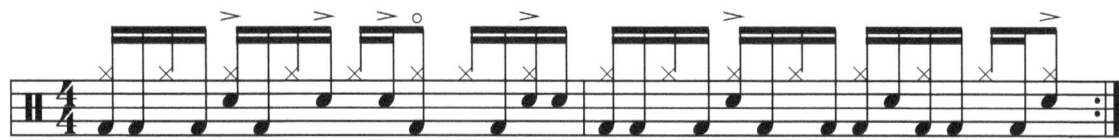

CLAVE GROOVES/RHYTHMIC STRUCTURE

283. With Bonham-esque tones.

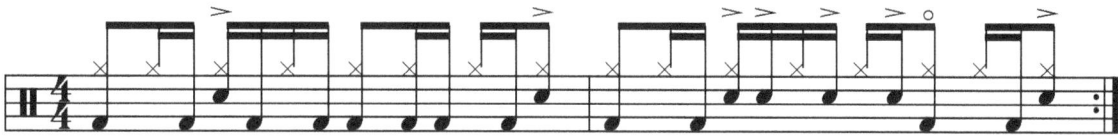

284.

285.

On the song "Neeps and Tatties" on the *Groove Alchemy* (Telarc Records, 2010) album, I draw from variations on "Look-Ka Py Py" for some parts of the tune, and "Whole Lotta Love" for others.

One of my favorite drummers from New Orleans, James Black, often used the concept of improvising over a rhythmic structure. Here's the main groove to Eddie Bo's "Hook and Sling." Notice that the groove is similar to the rhythmic structure of "Cold Sweat," but the first and second measures have been reversed. James improvises wildly throughout the tune, but keeps coming back to this groove.

286. "Hook and Sling" **Eddie Bo 1969, drums: James Black, c. 99 bpm.**

This one has a lot of tambourine in the mix, so let's try playing it with a jingle stick in the right hand.

Now let's examine the rhythmic structure.

277.

CLAVE GROOVES/RHYTHMIC STRUCTURE

Again we can start to come up with variations based on the stripped-down structure. Here's one that adds Clyde's chatter notes.

288. c. 99 bpm

Add Jabo's skip beats on the hi-hat.

289.

You can vary the rhythmic structure slightly and ornament the backbeat further to create more variations as well.

290.

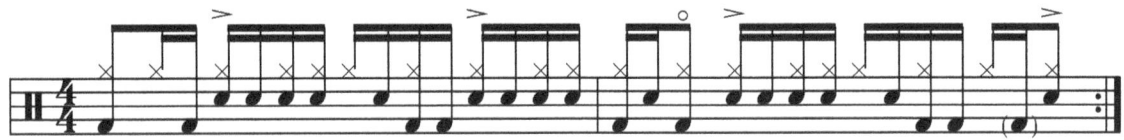

Here's a groove James Black played on the Inell Young tune "The Next Ball Game." Again James improvises throughout the tune, making it hard to pick one bar as the main groove.

Here is an approximation of the main groove.

291. "The Next Ball Game" Inell Young 1969, drums: James Black, c. 110 bpm.

What I like about this rhythmic structure is that the 3 side of the clave appears in the middle of the bar, starting with the backbeat on beat 2.

292.

CLAVE GROOVES/RHYTHMIC STRUCTURE

We can ornament the backbeat by adding Clyde's chatter notes.

293. c. 110 bpm

Again we can add Jabo's skip beats.

294.

Adding some left-hand interjection on the hi-hat, á la Zig.

295. c. 100 bpm

Add in some buzzes.

296.

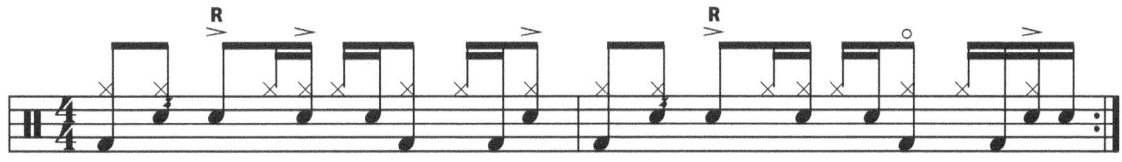

297.

CLAVE GROOVES/RHYTHMIC STRUCTURE

Even some of the more modern and syncopated grooves of Mike Clark and David Garibaldi have underlying rhythmic structures. Let's take another look at David's groove to the Tower of Power tune "Soul Vaccination."

298. "Soul Vaccination" *Tower of Power* 1973, drums: David Garibaldi, c. 106 bpm.

Although the groove is seemingly very syncopated and complex, my ear locks into the underlying rhythm of:

299.

Check out pages 65-67 for variations on this rhythmic structure.

Here are some more grooves with rhythmic structures that I've found useful.

300.

I play the following groove on the Galactic tune "Baker's Dozen" and the Garage à Trois song "The Dwarf."

301.

302.

CLAVE GROOVES/RHYTHMIC STRUCTURE

303.

304.

305. c. 110 bpm

306.

307.

308.

CLAVE GROOVES/RHYTHMIC STRUCTURE

309.

310.

These start to vary that structure by leaving out the 1 of the second measure.

I play ideas similar to this one on the tune "Late Night at the Maple Leaf" on my Trio record *Emphasis!* (*On Parenthesis*). Some of these are loose interpretations of some of Mike Clark-style ideas as well.

311.

312.

These vary the structure by leaving out the 1 of the first measure.

313.

314.

CLAVE GROOVES/RHYTHMIC STRUCTURE

These vary the structure a bit further in the second measure.

315.

316.

These next examples are coming from what I'd call a "double backbeat" groove. This is where the snare plays two consecutive eighth notes on beat 2 to create a kind of double backbeat on beat 2. This groove can be incredibly funky and slinky, or can be straightened out and sped up a bit to create a surf beat. Let's examine some double backbeat grooves. This first rhythmic structure is two bars and has a double backbeat in the first bar and a regular backbeat in the second bar. You could reverse the order of the bars to come up with more variations as well.

317.

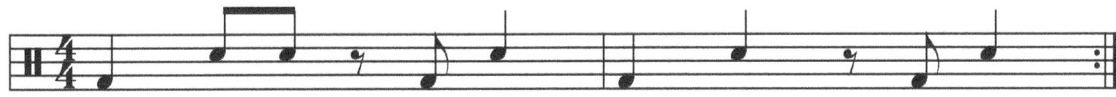

These first three work well if you place the right hand around the kit on different sound sources.

318.

319.

CLAVE GROOVES/RHYTHMIC STRUCTURE

320.

You could throw in some Clyde Stubblefield...

321.

You could vary the structure slightly by leaving out the 1 of the second measure.

322.

Let's throw in some ideas from the "Zig Exploration" we examined previously.

323. c. 96 bpm

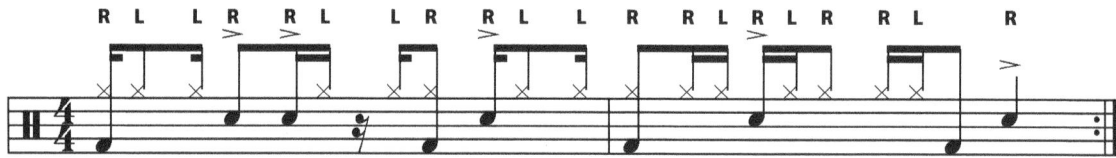

This next rhythmic structure is one bar with a double backbeat in each bar, but you can still get a two-bar groove happening.

324.

CLAVE GROOVES/RHYTHMIC STRUCTURE

325.

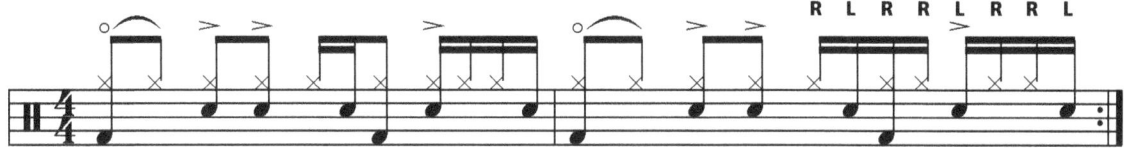

Here's a version of one of my favorite grooves that I picked up from Johnny Vidacovich.

326.

Again, you can start to throw in some Clyde.

327.

328.

Here's one that throws in some of the "Zig Exploration" again.

329. c. 96 bpm

CLAVE GROOVES/RHYTHMIC STRUCTURE

Elvin Jones often used rhythmic structures in a jazz context as well. He can often be heard playing over the clave. Check out his playing on "Equinox" off the John Coltrane record *The Sound of John Coltrane*. Even though he's improvising throughout the tune, what he plays stays locked into the underlying clave. Elvin would use this concept on other tunes as well. I heard him play at the New Orleans Jazz Festival a few years before he passed. The first tune he did was played with this clave as the predominate rhythmic structure.

330.

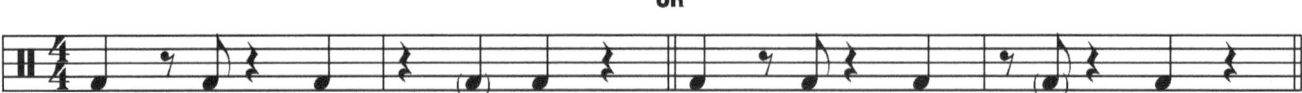

I'll improvise over this rhythmic structure in a style reminiscent of Elvin.

331. AUDIO ONLY

I've also seen Elvin play over this rhythmic structure...

332.

Again, I'll improvise over this structure.

333. AUDIO ONLY

Brian Blade also uses the concept of improvising over the clave in a jazz context to great effect on the Kenny Garret record *Pursuance, the Music of John Coltrane*. Check out his interpretations of "Equinox" and "Lonnie's Lament."

I find the concept of rhythmic structures to be very useful when approaching odd time signatures as well. Whenever I play in an odd meter, I first try to figure out what the repeating underlying rhythmic structure is. This helps me lock into what's going on musically and also helps keep me from having to count every bar.

When playing in 5, most tunes usually lock into this structure.

334.

CLAVE GROOVES/RHYTHMIC STRUCTURE

Let's check out some grooves over this.

335.

336.

337.

You can put the right hand on the snare and modify some of the stickings from *Take It To The Street* for some "second line" grooves in 5.

338.

339.

340.

CLAVE GROOVES/RHYTHMIC STRUCTURE

You can move the right hand to the cowbell. These sound good with the handbourine in the right hand on the cowbell as well.

341.

342.

You can syncopate things a bit to make things a little more interesting.

Here's a rhythmic structure James Black played off in later versions of his tune "Magnolia Triangle."

343.

Let's try some grooves based on this structure.

344.

345.

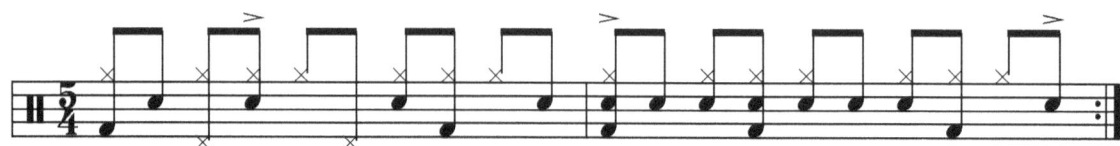

CLAVE GROOVES/RHYTHMIC STRUCTURE

Let's try to get some street beat ideas.

346.

You can start to vary the stickings as well.

347.

348.

349.

I've found the following structure very helpful when playing grooves in 7.

350.

CLAVE GROOVES/RHYTHMIC STRUCTURE

And here are some grooves over that.

351.

Here's one that incorporates some of Clyde's chatter notes.

352.

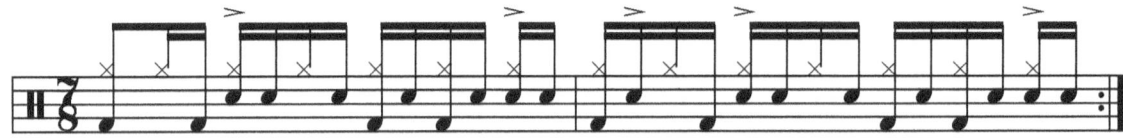

This one is basically a 7/8 version of Jabo's groove to "Sex Machine."

353.

Here's one that blends Clyde and Jabo in 7.

354.

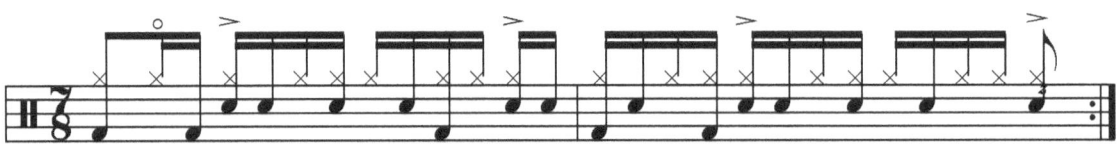

And finally one reminiscent of Zig, in 7.

355.

CLAVE GROOVES/RHYTHMIC STRUCTURE

Whenever I improvise on or vary the grooves that I'm playing, I try to keep the underlying structure present. This helps keep what I'm playing musically relevant and coherent. Let's check out the following musical example. I'll start with the simple structure of 1 on the bass with 2 and 4 on the snare. As I start to improvise on the groove, I'll stay true to the structure at hand. This will keep things related to the groove at hand and will hopefully keep the listener's attention and keep what I'm playing from sounding like it's rambling or directionless.

356.

Check out this audio example with the preceding underlying rhythmic structure.

357. AUDIO ONLY 32 bars total.

Again we can self-edit and pick out several ideas to loop or repeat. You can take a mental snapshot while you're playing, you could stop and write the good ideas down, or you could record yourself and pick out the key spots and make them into grooves.

Let's check out what happens when I actually loop several of the ideas I came up with and write them out.

358. Looped from bars 7 and 8.

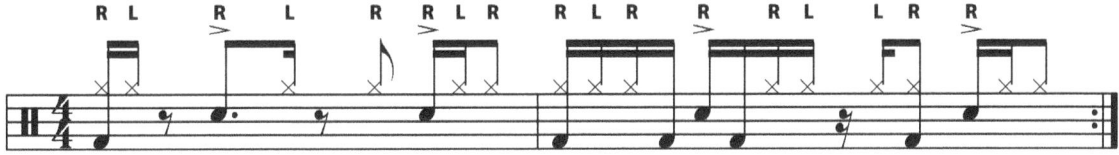

359. Looped from bars 15 and 16.

360. Looped from bars 20 and 21.

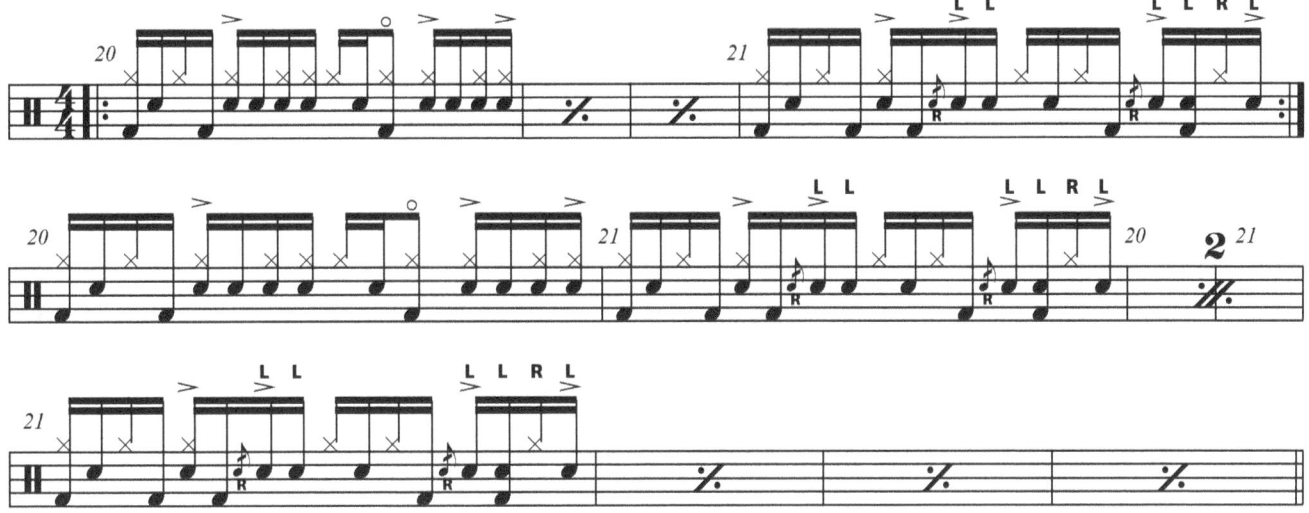

SWING/SHUFFLES

SWING

I think it's very important to understand swing (at least in some capacity) to fully understand groove. To me, swing is a groove just like any other, it's just more subtle and is played with its own set of nuances. The pulse (or underlying rhythmic structure) is the quarter note. It's important to be able to make the quarter note feel good, groove, and swing. Often we'll hear the question, "Is it swinging?" This can be a perplexing question with elusive answers. To me all this means is, Is it grooving? Does it feel good? I think there is often a lot of emphasis on coordination when younger drummers first start getting interested in learning jazz. I thinks it is ever more important to concentrate on developing a strong time feel that grooves and swings. Once you have a strong groove with good time and a good feel, you can add all the coordination and intricacies. First you must have a strong foundation, just like in building a house. Once your foundation is solid, then you can add the rest of your structure. You wouldn't want to install granite countertops and gold-plated faucets in a house built on sand…right?

A lot of the drummers that we consider to be the greatest groove players—Earl Palmer, Zigaboo Modeliste, John Bonham, Steve Jordan, John "Jabo" Starks—grew up hearing jazz and music that swung. They were all raised on Big Band jazz, bebop, blues, rhythm and blues, early rock 'n' roll—all music based in swing. To be able to really groove, I think it's important to be able to swing. With swing, it's not enough to just play the notes. You have to make the notes feel good and groove.

THE IMPORTANCE OF THE QUARTER NOTE

When I started playing jazz and first started swinging, knowing exactly what to do to make things swing was often an elusive concept. Once I had the epiphany that the swing lay in the quarter notes, my groove improved immensely. This was an eye- and ear-opening revelation. Once I started listening to Jimmy Cobb on Miles Davis' *Kind of Blue*, I started to understand swing a great deal more. It's possible to play quarter notes with such conviction and soul, they move and swing the band in a way that leaves the listener wanting to hear nothing else. The trick is to find the balance. You have to understand how to play a strong quarter-note pulse that is still supple and subtle at the same time. All you have to do to discover this is listen to "Freddie Freeloader" over and over again, and you will to start to understand the importance of the quarter note. Even though Jimmy is adding skip beats, the quarter note is always there. Once you can swing the band and make people want to dance just by playing quarter notes, everything else will start to fall into place.

SWING/SHUFFLES

Try the following two examples while playing along to "Freddie Freeloader."

361.

362. Accenting 2 & 4 can sometimes add forward motion.

The Jazz Ride Cymbal Pattern

Once you start playing the jazz ride cymbal pattern, there are points of emphasis to consider. Some people feel that accenting the pattern on 2 and 4 makes the ride cymbal pattern swing harder. This should sound like lang SPANG-a lang SPANG-a lang or tie TIE your tie TIE your tie.

363.

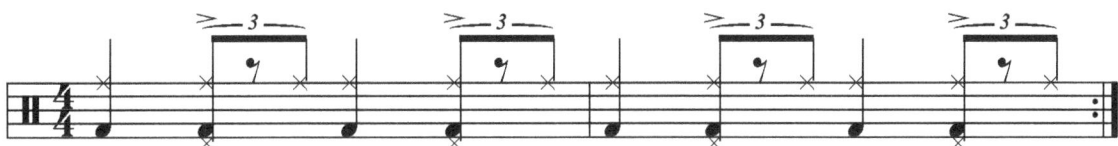

Others feel that putting an emphasis on the skip beat gives motion to the feel and makes it swing harder. This is sometimes referred to as an "upbeat swing." Elvin Jones is a known proponent of this style: lang spang-A lang spang-A lang.

364.

GROOVE ALCHEMY

SWING/SHUFFLES

You can also experiment with accenting the 2 and 4 and the skip beat as well: lang SPANG-A lang SPANG-A lang.

365.

Very rarely, if ever, would you want to put emphasis on beat 1... maybe when playing the pattern on the hi-hat. Even then I would emphasize it as LANG spang-A LANG spang-A LANG.

366.

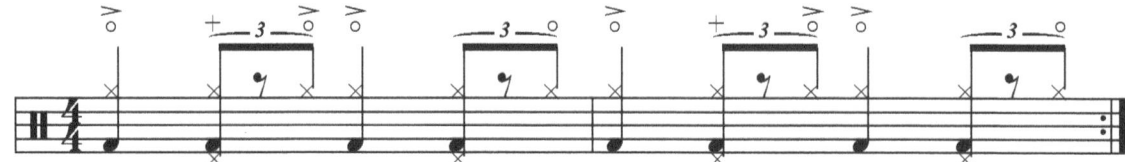

You definitely *don't* want to do this...

367. Intentionally played badly to demonstrate what not to do.

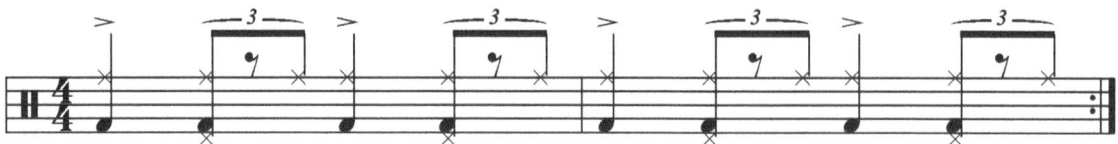

I recommend experimenting with all of these (except the *don't* version) and getting comfortable with each. Through much listening, you'll be able to determine which feel will be appropriate for the musical situation at hand.

SWING/SHUFFLES

Phrasing the Skip Beat

Another element to consider is how to phrase the skip beat or how much to swing the eighth notes. Even though swing eighth notes are often written as regular straight eighth notes, in general swing eighth notes are phrased...

368.

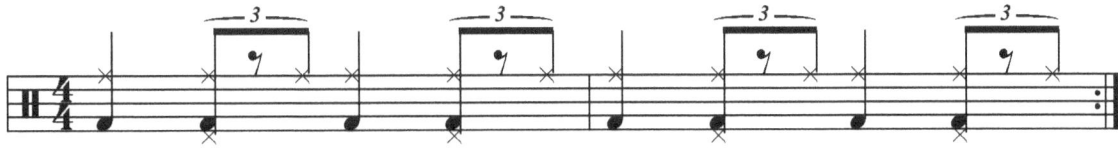

or

369.

Often they are phrased somewhere in-between the two.

As the tempo increases, it is common to let the eighth note straighten out a bit. That starts to look like this...

370.

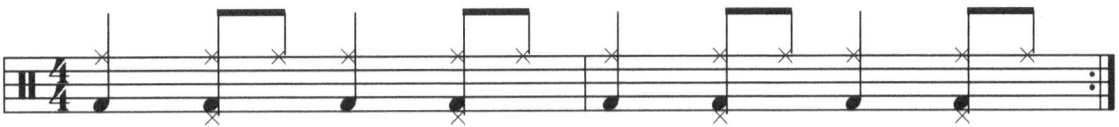

Conversely, at slower tempos it is common to open up the space between beats 2 and 4 and the skip beat. That looks like this...

371.

or

372.

SWING/SHUFFLES

In general the skip beat seems to want to be closer to the note directly following it. You want to find where the placement of the skip beat feels right for you at many different tempos. Extensive listening to the great jazz drummers will help you develop a greater understanding of where you want to place your skip beats and how you want to phrase your ride cymbal pattern. Everyone has their own way of playing the ride cymbal beat, so you want to listen and experiment to find out what works for you.

Morphing the Ride Cymbal Pattern

Let's try morphing the skip beat at eight different tempos. I'll start by phrasing the skip beat where I like to place it, then I'll morph it more towards swing, to the point of too swung. I'll then morph it toward too straight. I'll end by playing back where I feel it.

Let's start at a medium tempo.

373. AUDIO 120 bpm

Now let's double that.

374. AUDIO 240 bpm

Now let's half the original 120.

375. AUDIO 60 bpm

Notice that all of these are based off of 60 bpm, or the ticking of the second hand on a wristwatch. You should practice finding all of these tempos with a wristwatch or by watching the second hand (or the digital blinking) of a wall or desk clock.

Once you get comfortable with those, you should be able to lock into 60 bpm. Next play sixteenth notes. Accent every third one. This will give you 80 bpm. From there you can find 160 bpm and 320 bpm by doubling and quadrupling 80.

376. AUDIO 80 bpm

377. AUDIO 160 bpm

378. AUDIO 320 bpm

From 60 bpm you can play sextuplets. If you accent every fourth sextuplet you will find 90 bpm. You can find 180 bpm from there by doubling that as well.

379. AUDIO 90 bpm
380. AUDIO 180 bpm

Experiment with moving the skip beat around at different tempos and listen to how great drummers phrase the skip beat. Try to notice for example how Tony Williams and Max Roach tend to phrase a bit straighter, while Elvin Jones and Brian Blade tend to phrase more on the swing side of the spectrum.

SWING/SHUFFLES

BRIEF HISTORY OF THE RIDE CYMBAL PATTERN

The ride cymbal pattern seems to have developed around the beginning of the 1900s. In the earliest forms of jazz, time was played on the snare drum & bass drum. The grooves that were played were often modified marches. With the advent of the bass drum pedal around 1909, these marches were eventually adapted to be played by one person instead of by a separate bass drummer and snare drummer. Notice that these are all coming from the five-stroke roll, which has a natural ebb and flow built into it. There's call and response, yin yang, up down, back forth, in out, and so on already built in. There is plenty more about this in my first book *Take It To The Street*. Some of these simplified marches looked like this…

381.

382.

383. R on snare, L on snare

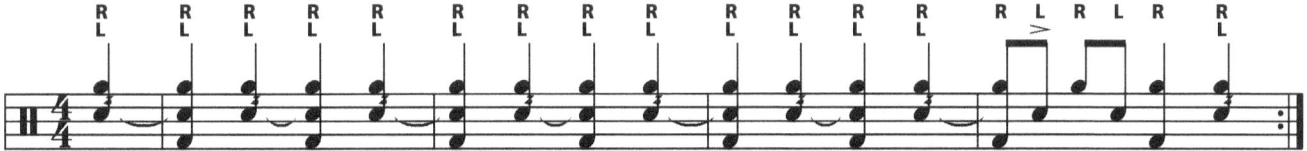

384. R on snare, L on snare

Let's check out a tune where the time is swung on the snare drum. The feel of this tune is intentionally loose and laid back.

385. "Keep On Gwine" FULL MIX

SWING/SHUFFLES

By the late 1920's and '30s, drummers (namely Baby Dodds) began moving the time up to the cymbals on the drum set to create a more legato and lighter texture. As the right hand began playing time on what became the ride cymbal (at that time cymbals were much smaller), drummers started adding the skip beat to fill out the time and make it more fluid. This developed into what we know as the jazz ride cymbal pattern. Also the pulse on the bass drum moved from 1 and 3 to all fours...again to make the time flow more effortlessly.

386.

387.

Eventually the backbeat was left off the snare in an effort to smooth out and elongate the time even further. When the lowboy was eventually introduced in the late '20s by the Ludwig Drum Company, it eventually evolved into the hi-hat which replaced the snare on 2 and 4. This started to look more like what we know as "jazz time" or the traditional jazz ride cymbal pattern.

388.

It's also interesting to note that ex. 387 was played during the ending or "shout" choruses at the end of jazz and Big Band tunes for years. Eventually Earl Palmer and others started playing that beat and variations thereof throughout the bulk of the tune in a new genre of music that eventually became "rock 'n' roll." Earl did this in the Fats Domino tune "The Fat Man," and many believe this to be the first "rock 'n' roll" song.

Check out this audio example that develops from a simple European/Civil War march into what has now become the ride cymbal pattern...

389. AUDIO ONLY

SWING/SHUFFLES

FEATHERING THE BASS DRUM

There's been a lot of debate over the years as to whether or not to play the bass drum on quarter notes when swinging. Traditionally, the bass drum was usually played on quarter notes in a swing context. As more methods became available to make the upright bass audible, the bass drum was played softer and softer, since you could now hear the bass and the bass drum was not providing all of the low end. So by the late forties (in early be-bop), guys were still playing the bass drum on all fours, even though they were also dropping bombs; they were just playing it softer, in a way that allowed you to feel it more than hear it. This technique is called feathering the bass drum. I think it's important to be able to feather the bass drum, whether you use it or not. It actually takes a good bit of control to be able to feather the bass drum in a way that feels good, especially at quicker tempos. A good place to start is to play quarter notes on the ride cymbal, while feathering the bass drum on quarter notes. Make sure to play very lightly with the heel down. Once you get comfortable with that, play the hi-hat on 2 and 4. When you're comfortable with that you can start adding the skip beat, which creates the traditional jazz ride cymbal pattern.

This technique comes in handy for Big Band and more traditional forms of jazz and swing. Once you understand feathering, the music will dictate when to use it.

SHUFFLES

I feel that it is very important to be able to play a solid shuffle in order to fully understand groove and swing. To me, the shuffle is a perfect combination of groove and swing. Being able to play a good shuffle will help you understand swing. It will also help your ability to groove.

The standard shuffle looks like this…

390.

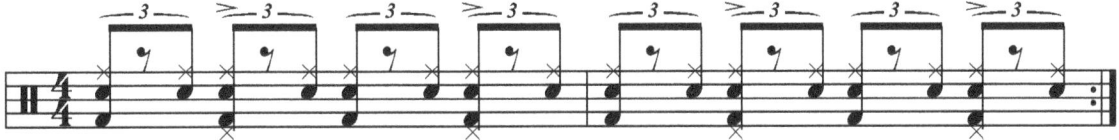

I think it is paramount to not just play the notes, but to understand and play the nuances that make this groove swing. Some players (especially Art Blakey) emphasize the snare drum note right before 2 and 4 almost as much as the 2 and 4 itself. Also I like to play the bass drum quietly (almost feathered) and put a slight emphasis on beats 2 and 4. As for the phrasing of the eighth notes, I personally like to swing them slightly more than the standard triplet notation would suggest. I would suggest experimenting with how much swing you put on the eighth notes.

Check out the following example. This is one of the ways I like to phrase the shuffle. It looks something like this:

391.

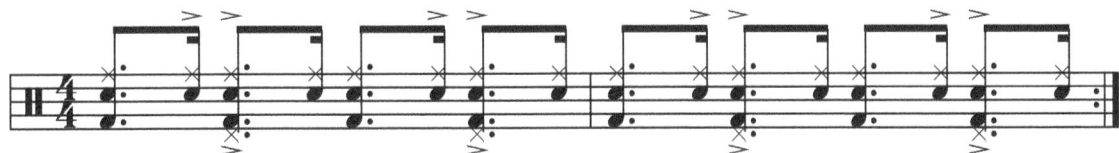

SWING/SHUFFLES

Now let's check out the shuffle without the inflections suggested. To me, the inflections make the shuffle swing and groove much harder.

392. AUDIO ONLY Same as 391, but played without inflections and intentionally played badly to demonstrate what not to do.

Morphing the Shuffle

So now, let's morph the shuffle as we have done with other grooves so far. We'll start off where I like to feel it. I'll then morph more toward the swing end of the spectrum, all the way past the point of good taste. I'll then morph it back where it should be. I'll then straighten it out till it's too straight. I'll end by bringing it back to where I feel it. The point of this is so that you can control the phrasing of the shuffle and you can determine how to phrase it for the musical situation at hand.

393. AUDIO ONLY

Once you get comfortable with the double shuffle (both hands shuffling), you should work on playing the shuffle with the jazz ride cymbal pattern.

394.

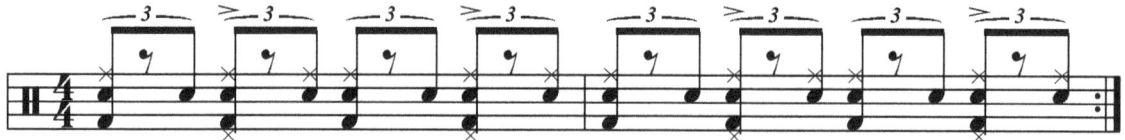

You should work on the shuffle with quarter notes in the right hand as well. I find this version of the shuffle grooves like mad, and I often use it as my "go to" shuffle.

395.

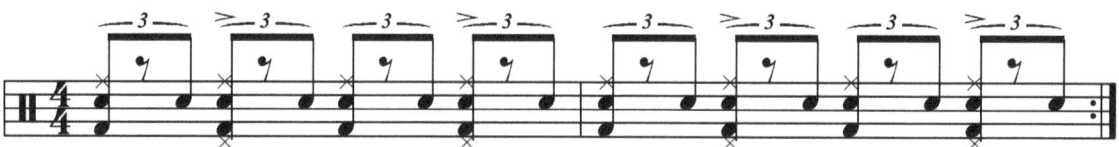

Let's check out some shuffle variations. Once you get comfortable playing the preceding shuffles with the three different patterns in the right hand (shuffled eighths, the jazz ride pattern, and quarter notes), you can vary the bass drum a bit. Let's start with a mambo bass drum pattern. Again, play all of these the three different ways with the right hand.

396.

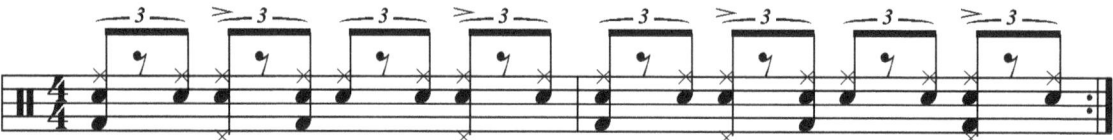

SWING/SHUFFLES

This one has upbeat eighth notes on the bass drum and has kind of a "backward" shuffle feel.

397.

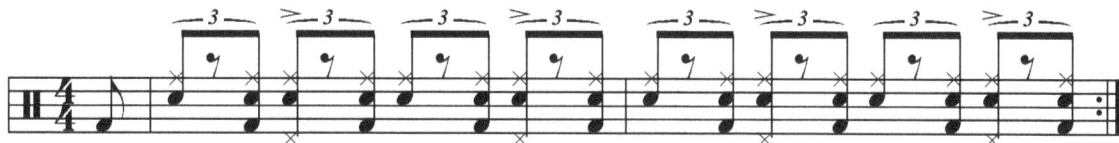

These next few leave off the 1 and 3 on the snare drum and work great for faster tempos. These start to creep into a swing version of Clyde Stubblefield's chatter notes.

398.

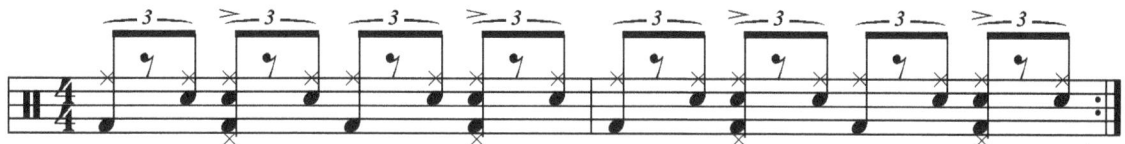

399.

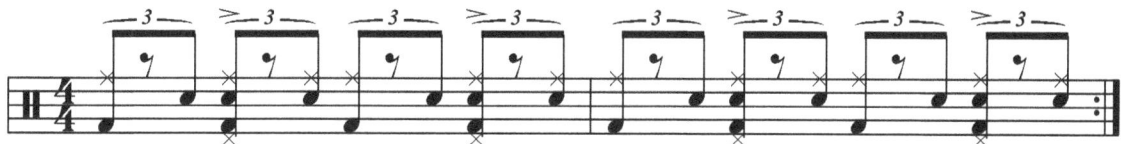

400.

Once again, when you get comfortable with these, try varying the bass drum.

Here's quarter notes in the right hand with the mambo-ish bass drum.

401.

SWING/SHUFFLES

And here's one with the jazz ride pattern in the right hand with the upbeat eighth notes on the bass.

402.

Here's a groove reminiscent of what Earl Palmer played on many early rock 'n' roll hits by Fats Domino and Little Richard. This is basically coming from a beefed-up shout chorus of a Big Band tune.

403.

Earl later added the mambo bass drum to this groove as well. There's more on Earl and his style of playing in *Take It To The Street*.

404.

The great Al Jackson Jr. played the following simplified shuffle on Booker T. and the MGs' hit "Green Onions." This groove often gets misinterpreted but, if played correctly, grooves like mad.

405. "Green Onions" Booker T. & The MGs *Green Onions* 1962, drums: Al Jackson Jr., c. 134 bpm.

This next one works great for a breakdown. You can also try it with a muted tone on the ride. This is achieved by actually pressing the tip of the right stick into the ride cymbal.

406. Play the audio example on open ride, then muted ride.

GROOVE ALCHEMY

SWING/SHUFFLES

It works great on the hi-hat…

407.

…and on the snare as well. A great New Orleans drummer by the name of Johnny Thomassie used to play shuffles similar to this one. When he played, it grooved like crazy.

408.

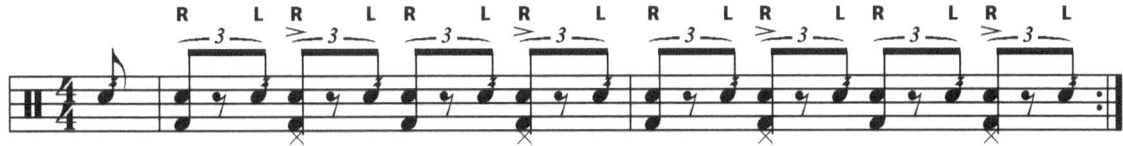

Here's one I use anytime I need to play a "backward" shuffle. The backward shuffle is when the guitar or piano is playing constant upbeat swing eighth notes.

409. c. 135 bpm

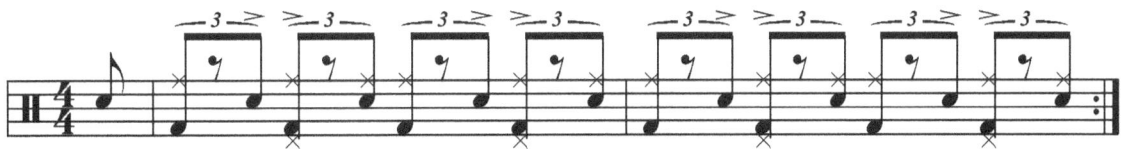

These next few work great at faster tempos. Since we're dealing with faster tempos and the notes will be straightened out a bit, I've written these in eighth notes.

410. c. 197 bpm

Again, this works great with the mambo bass drum pattern.

411.

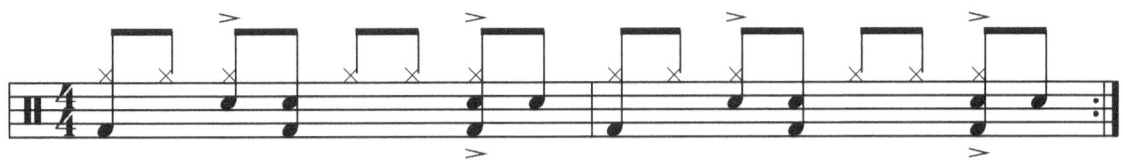

SWING/SHUFFLES

These work great with the right hand on the hi-hat or snare as well.

Here it is written out with the right hand on the snare and the mambo bass drum pattern on the bass drum. When the hands play together, they should be played as left-handed flams. This works great for a train beat or snare drum shuffle.

412.

Here's a heavier shuffle, the likes of which was pioneered by Bill Ward in Black Sabbath. This groove works great in heavier situations. You can crash the ride, making this as heavy as you want to make it. I played this groove on the Corrosion of Conformity tune "Stonebreaker" from *In the Arms of God*. If played crashing on the ride and with a 26-inch bass drum, this groove is *heavy*. Part of why I got the call to do that record was because they knew I could make heavy grooves like this also *swing*.

413.

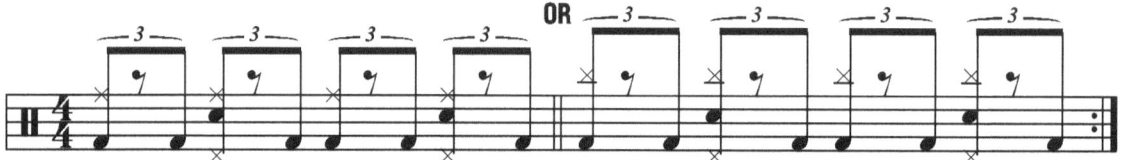

SWING/SHUFFLES

Let's talk about the upbeat hi-hat shuffle. This beat was pioneered by Philadelphia drummer Donald Bailey during his stint with the great organist Jimmy Smith. Donald's playing helped define a vocabulary and approach to playing the drums with organ combos. Let's start by looking at Donald's groove to the Jimmy Smith classic "Back At The Chicken Shack."

414. "Back At The Chicken Shack" **Jimmy Smith 1960, drums: Donald Bailey, c. 111 bpm.**

This style of shuffle was further developed and popularized by Steve Gadd, who also had a lot of experience playing in organ combos. Let's check out these Steve Gadd shuffles. These can be played with the right hand on the hi-hat (as written) or on the ride.

415. c. 125 bpm

416.

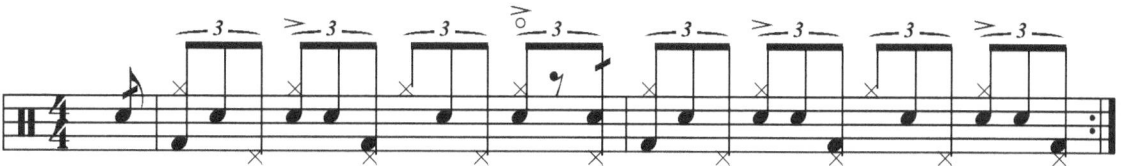

417.

Try playing these with the right hand playing all the hi-hat notes. This may help smooth some of these ideas out, and help them to groove on a deeper level.

SWING/SHUFFLES

While we're on the topic of shuffles, I'd like to cover some double bass drum shuffles as well. This type of shuffle was popularized by Billy Cobham, Simon Phillips, Terry Bozzio, and Alex Van Halen. Let's start by re-examining example 397. Let's now play straight quarter notes on the hi-hat with the left foot instead of 2 and 4. Now move the left foot from the hi-hat to the double pedal, and you're playing a double bass drum shuffle.

418. c. 180 bpm

Note that these are generally played at much faster tempos than regular shuffles. I often like to play these with my left foot on my 20-inch bass drum with my right on the 26-inch bass drum for the upbeats.

Also note that with the upbeat hi-hat shuffle, the left foot is obviously playing the upbeats. With the double bass drum shuffle, however, it is common to play the upbeats with the right foot. This is because the right foot is usually more used to playing upbeats whereas the left foot is used to playing quarter notes on the hi-hat. This makes it easier to get the double bass drum shuffle up and running and also makes it easier when trying to add ideas on top of the feet.

Since there is so much going on with these types of shuffles, you would usually simplify the hands a bit. Check these out.

419.

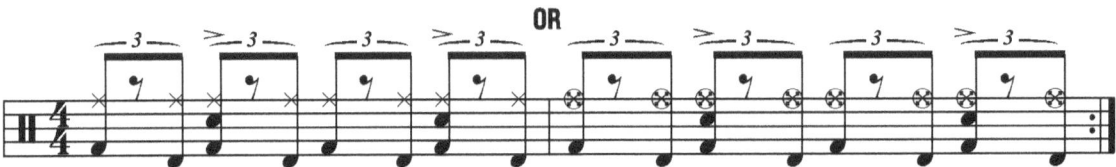

420. c. 200 bpm

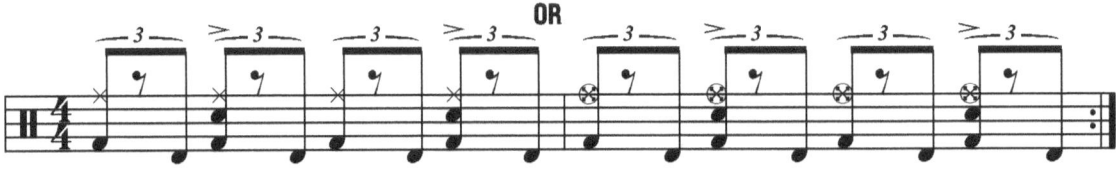

421.

You could fit most of the hand patterns from the previous shuffle examples over the double bass drum shuffle. Experiment and see what works for you.

GROOVE ALCHEMY

SWING/SHUFFLES

Here's the groove Alex Van Halen plays in the guitar intro to "Hot For Teacher."

422. "Hot For Teacher" intro groove, Van Halen *1984*, **1984, drums: Alex Van Halen, c. 256 bpm.**

20" b.d.
26" b.d.

He then simplifies to this...

423. "Hot For Teacher" main groove.

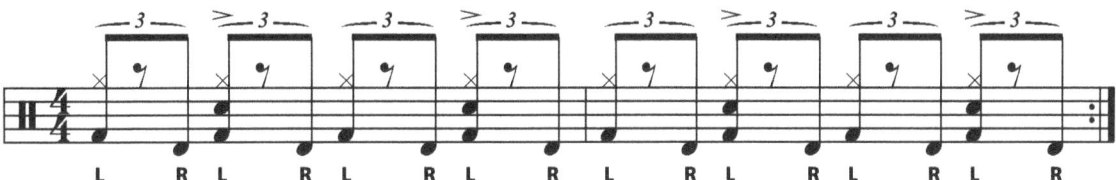

To make things more challenging, you can start to throw in Swiss triplets. You can play left-hand lead Swiss triplets over the double bass drum shuffle and accent every other one. This gives you diddles in the left hand and the shuffle ride pattern in the right.

424.

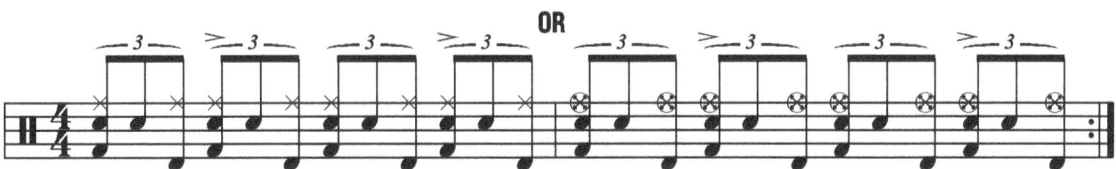

Here are some variations on that idea.

425.

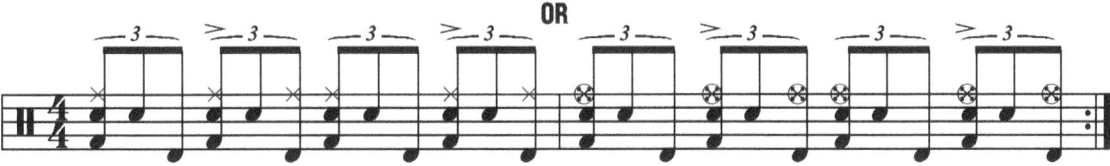

426.

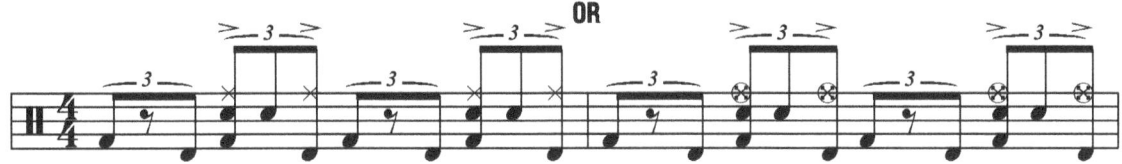

SWING/SHUFFLES

427.

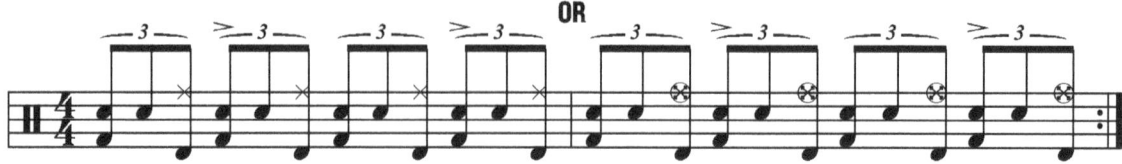

You could let the left foot straddle both the bass drum pedal and the hi-hat, and get some hit-hat barks as well.

428. c. 190 bpm

You can create a three-note phrase that works great for fills.

429.

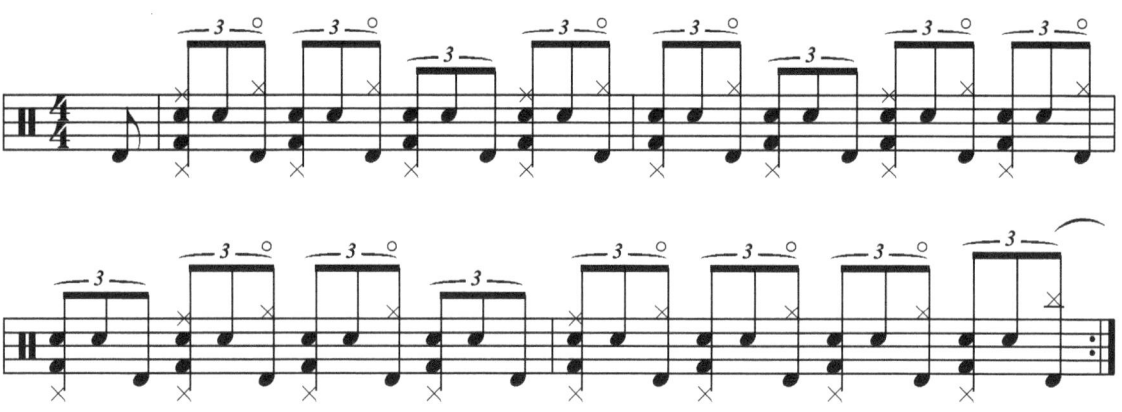

430.

SWING/SHUFFLES

Here's one that suggests a quarter-note triplet in the left hand, starting with the backbeat.

431.

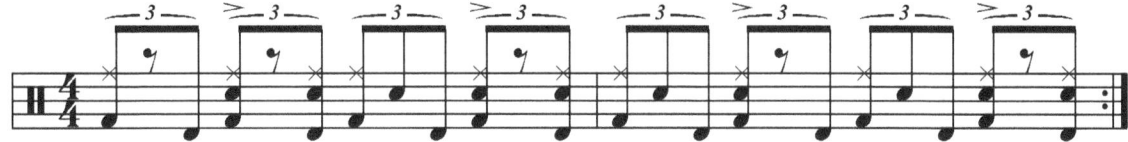

You can create a three-note phrase with this as well.

432.

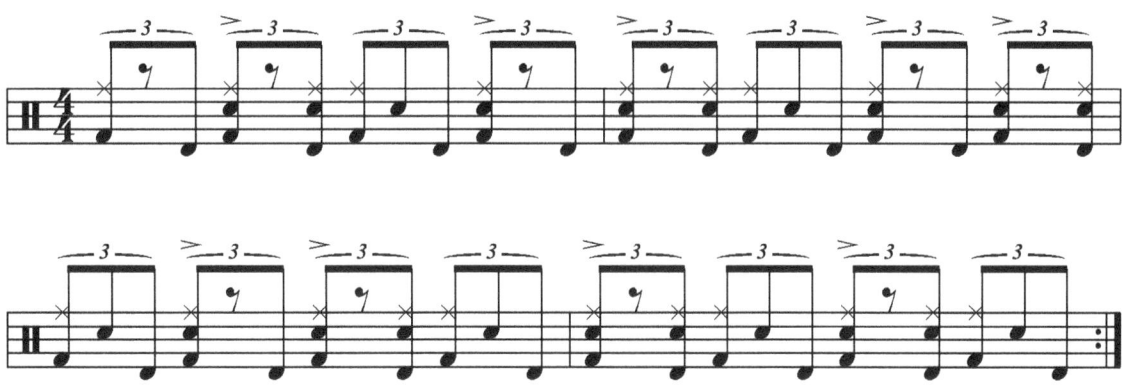

I spread this around the toms and use it as a fill idea all the time. Here it is written out as a sextuplet fill in a funk context without the left-foot bass drum, but you can simply move the left foot from the hi-hat to the left-foot bass drum pedal or straddle both the hi-hat and bass drum pedals. Some of these ideas can start to sound like there is a delay on the drums.

433.

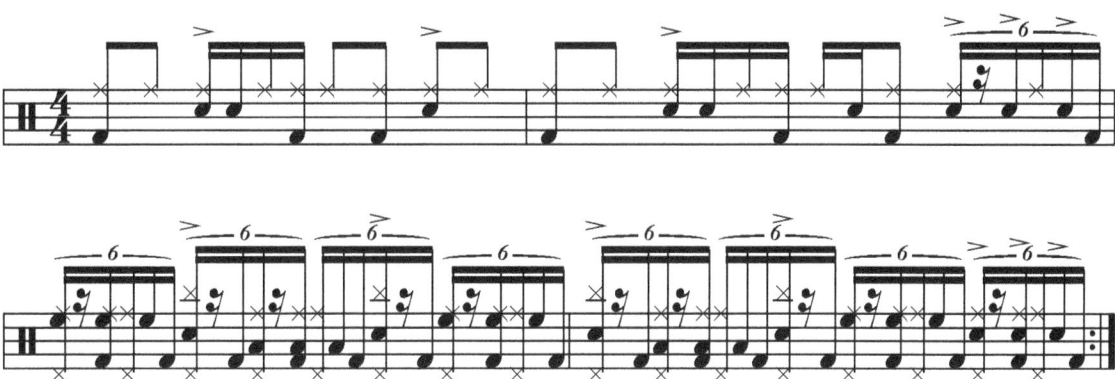

SWING/SHUFFLES

You could also play this idea with the left foot playing on 2 and 4 (if triplets) or upbeat eighth notes (if sextuplets).

434. c. 200 bpm or 100 bpm

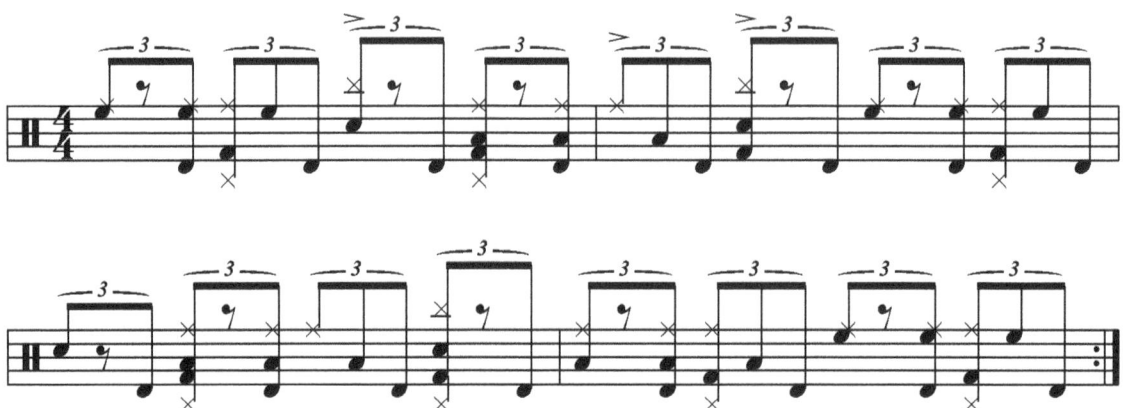

Here's that idea put into a fill.

435. AUDIO ONLY

Here are some that have more of a linear triplet feel. The hands play alternating right and left strokes and are split up between the hi-hat and snare. You can also try these with the right hand on the ride.

436. c. 118 bpm

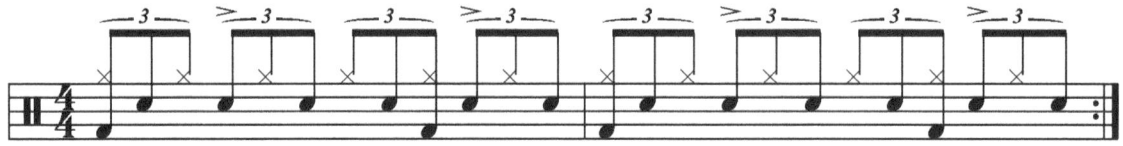

437.

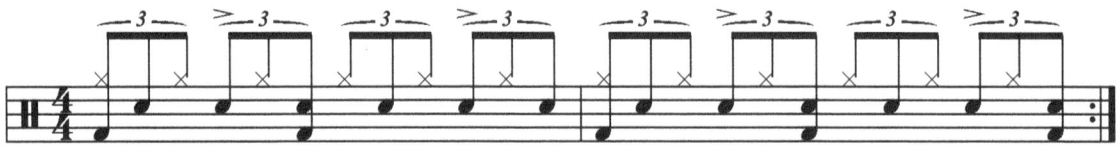

438.

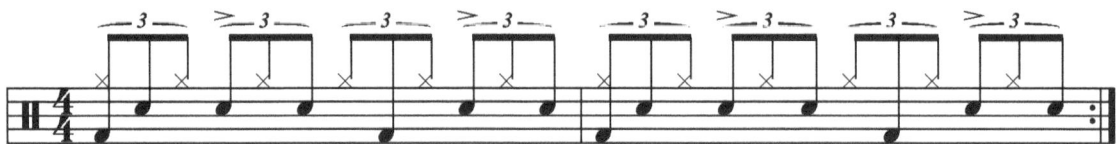

439.

SWING/SHUFFLES

I could write out shuffle variations for days. These are the main ones I've found useful. Check these out and spend some time with them. Also check out some of the music in the suggested listening to digest some of these grooves further. I strongly feel that some time spent swinging and learning to shuffle will go a long way to improve your groove.

Here's a tune with some of these shuffle ideas in it.

440. *"Up To Here"* **FULL MIX**

12/8 or SLOW 3

I'd like to talk a bit about the 12/8 groove. This is sometimes referred to as 6/8 or slow 3. It is often played for slow blues or triplet-based ballads. It's easy to overlook this groove because it is so deceptively simple. I think that spending some time with this groove though will deepen your pocket. It can help you develop patience, focus, and an appreciation for space. You should focus on placing every note exactly where it should be placed... especially the backbeat. It's important to try and lay the backbeat behind the beat with this one. Also, I like to generally play a lower-pitched snare drum on this.

These are written with the right hand on the ride but play these on the hi-hat as well.

441. c. 60 bpm

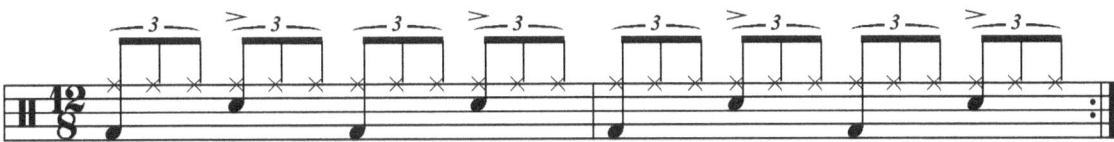

442.

443.

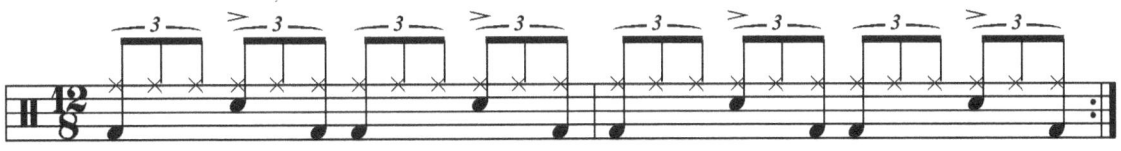

Earl Palmer added the skip beat to the right hand. Check these out.

444.

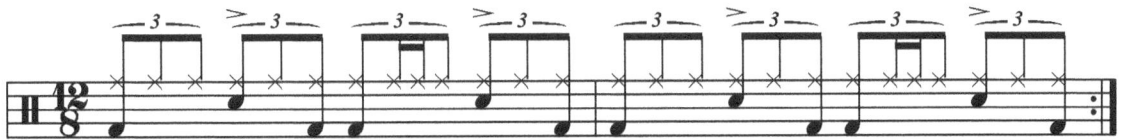

SWING/SHUFFLES

445.

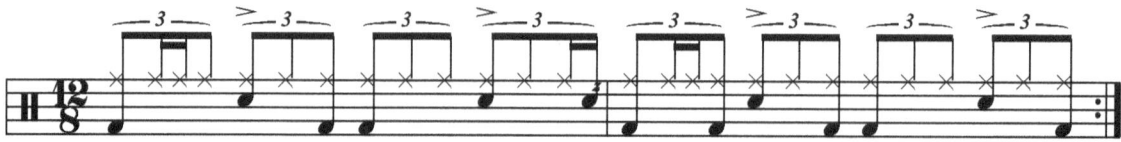

I like swishing the right hand with a brush on the floor tom or snare...

446.

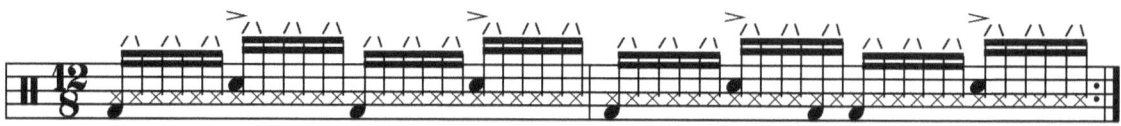

You can definitely get more complicated with these and I've seen plenty more elaborate variations. I like to keep these types of grooves simple though.

The Purdie Shuffle

No section on shuffles and triplet-based grooves would be complete without mention of the Purdie shuffle, also referred to as the half-time shuffle. Bernard demonstrates his classic groove very well in his video *Groove Master*. When played correctly these will sound like a cross between a shuffle, a funk groove, and a 12/8 all in one. Here are some to get started with.

447. "Home At Last" intro groove, Steely Dan *Aja* 1977, drums: Bernard Purdie, c. 64 bpm.

448. "Home At Last" chorus groove.

449. "Home At Last" outro groove.

SWING/SHUFFLES

450. "Babylon Sisters" intro groove, Steely Dan *Gaucho* 1980, drums: Bernard Purdie, c. 61 bpm.

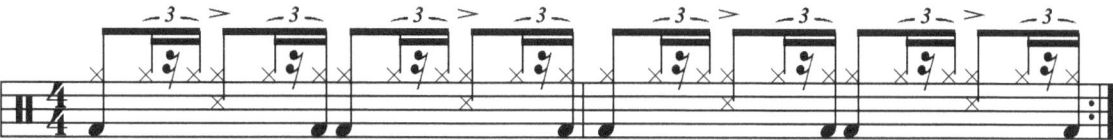

451. "Babylon Sisters" main groove.

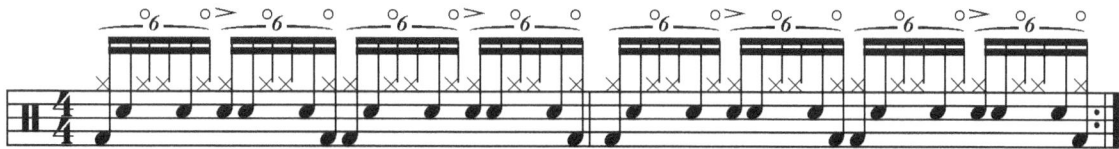

Bernard gets little mini "shoops" with the hi-hat. To achieve this, bounce your heel on the hi-hat in eighth notes. The ball of the foot stays compressed on the hi-hat. To get the "shoop," just lighten the pressure (ever so slightly) on the hi-hat pedal with the ball of your left foot. The "shoops" will start to creep out by themselves. Remember these should sound as effortless as possible. Make sure to listen to Bernard to really hear how to make these sound and feel right.

Of course John Bonham played his interpretation of the Purdie shuffle on "Fool In The Rain."

452. "Fool In The Rain" first two bars, Led Zeppelin *In Through The Out Door* 1979, drums: John Bonham, c. 65 bpm.

And Jeff Porcaro played his interpretation for "Rosanna."

453. "Rosanna" intro, Toto *Toto IV* 1982, drums: Jeff Porcaro, c. 86 bpm.

454. "Rosanna" main groove.

SWING/SHUFFLES

Here are some variations to try as well.

455. c. 72 bpm

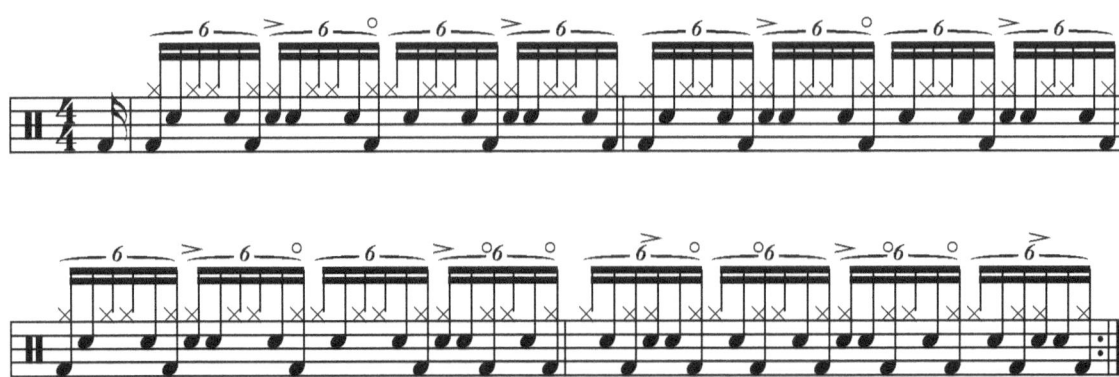

You could experiment with different stickings as well. Here's one based off a double paradiddle. Notice that the right hand spells out an Afro-Cuban bell pattern.

456.

Here's one based off a paradiddle-diddle.

457.

458.

These can be tricky to make feel right. Make sure to take your time and start off playing these slowly. Play to the metronome and make sure that every note is even and is laying where it should. If you concentrate on laying down the backbeat solidly and steadily, it will help the whole groove fall into place.

BACKBEATS

The backbeat started making appearances in the early 1900s when drummers (namely Baby Dodds) started moving the time from the snare drum press rolls up to the cymbal. The 2 and 4 were accented on the snare while the right hand played the ride cymbal pattern. This groove was used in shout choruses at the end of tunes in jazz, swing, and Big Band contexts. In the late '40s, as rock 'n' roll began to evolve from jump blues, the shout chorus groove and variations thereof started to become the primary groove throughout the entire tune.

Drummers (namely Earl Palmer with Fats Domino and Little Richard, and Fred Below with Chuck Berry) began experimenting with this new and powerful development. As rhythm and blues morphed into rock 'n' roll and soul morphed into funk, the backbeat continued to be an ever-present force in contemporary and popular music. To find out more about the history of the backbeat, check out Daniel Glass' book *The History of Rock 'n' Roll Drumming* and Steve Smith's DVD *Drumset Technique/History of the US Beat*.

The backbeat is the heartbeat of most contemporary music today. It is prevalent in rock, blues, swing, soul, funk, country, hip-hop, metal, polka, you name it. It may be simple, but it should never be taken for granted. I once read that Tony Williams referred to the backbeat as "the breath of God." It is often much harder to make a backbeat groove than people originally think.

In many grooves, the backbeat is the main event, the most important part of that groove. If you place it correctly within the groove, it can make all the other elements, both what you are playing on the drums and the other instruments you are playing with, fall into place. Its importance cannot be overstated.

The backbeat can be fine-tuned or altered in many ways to make or break a groove. You can use the following concepts to add life or interest to just about any backbeat groove.

PLACEMENT

There's been a lot of talk about playing on top of or behind the beat and about laying the backbeat on or behind the beat. I've found lots of backbeat grooves to feel best when the backbeat is laid back ever so slightly. Again, there are no rules. Stewart Copeland is one of my favorite drummers and most of his grooves push forward and still feel great.

You can begin to experiment with the placement of the backbeat by playing along to a metronome or record. You can begin to lay the backbeat back ever so slightly. I find it best to play the hi-hat in time and perhaps play the tightest of flams so that the left hand on the snare lands just after the right on the hi-hat or ride. This should be almost inaudible…more felt than heard. You can experiment with this concept and exaggerate how much you lay it back to see how to make it work for different situations. Make sure to record yourself to see what works and what doesn't.

I think you'll be doing yourself a disservice if you don't try this against some steady source of time. Most things these days are recorded to a click, loop, drum machine, or some sort of time source. You need to be able to do this with confidence while playing along to some sort of time. That said, you should also be able to do this on your own without leaning on a time source. You don't want to leave any limitations in your playing, if possible.

BACKBEATS

Once you've experimented with this, you should be able to comfortably lay the backbeat back in a way that will make the groove sit better. Sometimes (a lot of times) a bass player or some other instrument will be playing on top or ahead of what you are laying down. If you lay the backbeat back just a little bit, it can make things feel a lot fatter and funkier. It may feel strange at first, especially if you're hearing it in the headphones for the first time. I remember checking out Johnny Vidacovich once in a rehearsal with a Big Band. I was sitting behind the band between the bass player and the drums. The bass player was playing a bit on top and Johnny was laying the backbeat so far back it almost sounded wrong. The space between where they were each feeling the beat felt like the size of a canyon. But when I went out front of the band it sounded perfectly fat, round, and grooving. When I walked back behind the band again... the canyon was still there. Johnny was creating a big fat crevice for the band to lie in. Most of the time those little gaps disappear in the track once all the other instruments are in place, and the overall track will sound that much fuller.

Let's experiment with laying the backbeat back. This is exaggerated on purpose, just to see how far you can push it so you can learn what will work. I played this to a click and I strongly recommend you do the same when trying these.

Start by playing the backbeat on the click, then gradually lay it back further and further. Eventually, bring it back on the click again.

459. AUDIO ONLY

Ornamenting the Backbeat

There's a lot that can be done to ornament, decorate, or liven up the backbeat. You can start by taking the simplest of grooves and spice them up by applying some of the following concepts. You can then apply these concepts to virtually any backbeat grooves to vary them infinitely.

Let's take a look at the basic groove that we will be altering. We'll be concentrating on funk grooves, but try these concepts with shuffles, rock grooves, and any other types of grooves you may encounter.

460.

Snare Drum Chatter Notes

One of the most common and useful things we can do is add chatter notes or grace notes after, before, or in-between the backbeats. These first examples feature chatter notes á la Clyde Stubblefield. Of course we could write out thousands of variations on this, but these are just to give you an idea of what can be done to the backbeats of pre-existing grooves to vary them and help spurn creativity. I started out by demonstrating some of these alterations to the simple groove above, but make sure to apply these ideas to other grooves as well. There are also plenty of variations on chatter notes in previous sections of the book.

BACKBEATS

461.

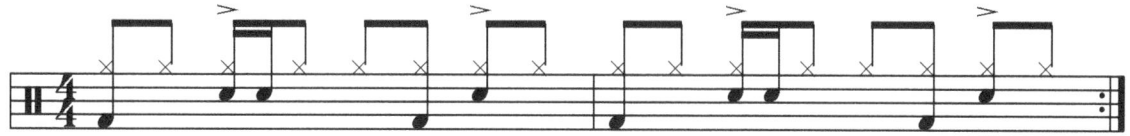

462.

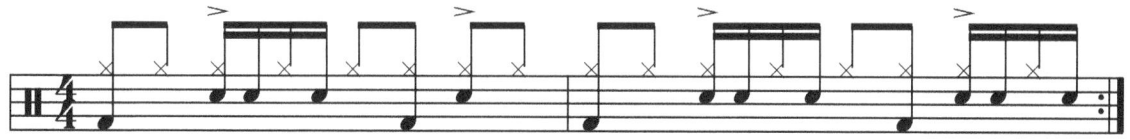

463.

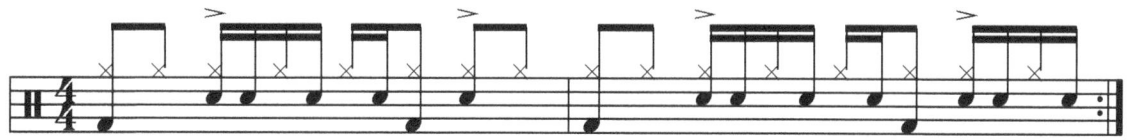

464.

465.

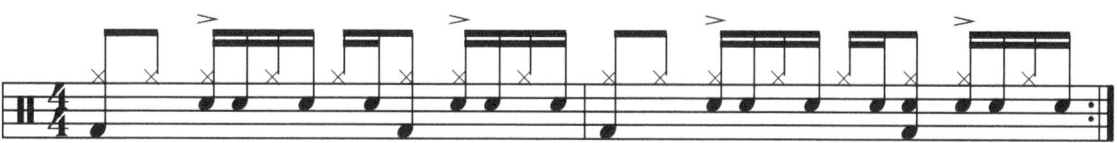

466.

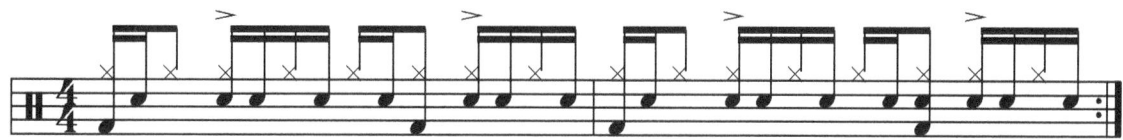

467.

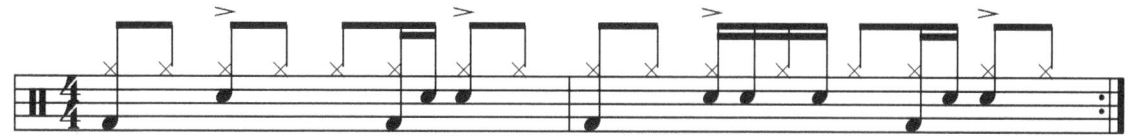

BACKBEATS

468.

469.

470.

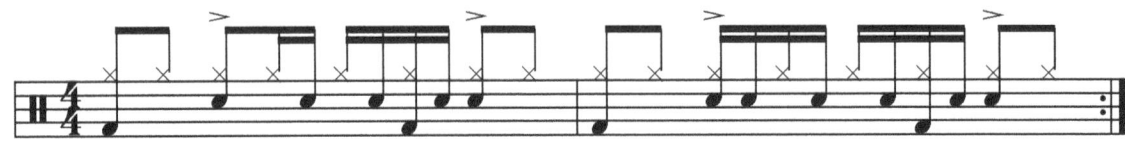

471.

472.

473.

GROOVE ALCHEMY

BACKBEATS

474.

475.

You can start to add accents and additional bass drum notes in strategic places to vary the original groove as well.

476.

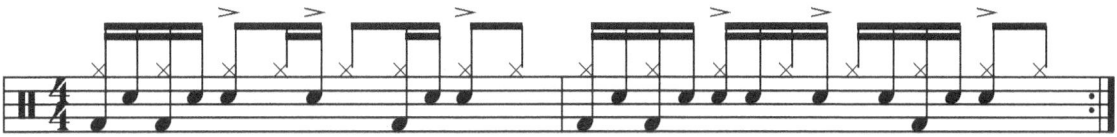

477.

478.

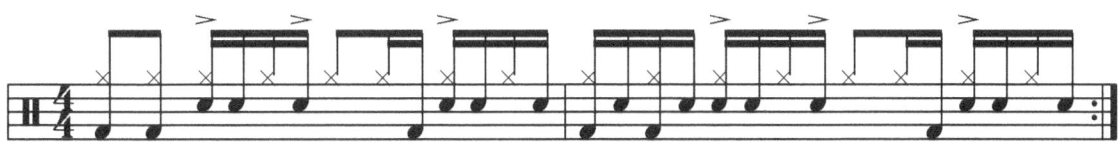

479.

BACKBEATS

You can add open hi-hat notes as well. These open hi-hat notes set the snare drum up to "snap."

480.

Again I could write out thousands of variations for days. I don't want to get too far off topic of what we can do to vary the actual backbeat. I'm just trying to give you some of the ideas that I've found to work, yet also leave room for you to come up with variations of your own.

Next let's start to add skip beats on the hi-hat, á la Jabo Starks.

481.

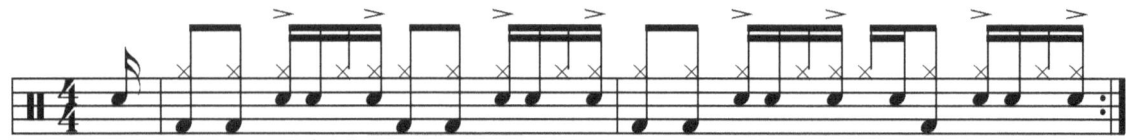

482.

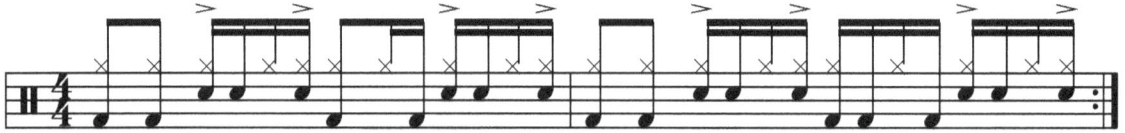

You can apply this concept with different rhythmic structures as well. Here's one with the "Cold Sweat" rhythmic structure.

483.

BACKBEATS

These next examples start to add in the recurring right-hand pattern that is basically the jazz ride cymbal pattern. This right-hand rhythm has been used to great effect by Bernard Purdie.

484.

485.

These next few utilize four consecutive notes on the snare…three chatter notes following the backbeat.

486.

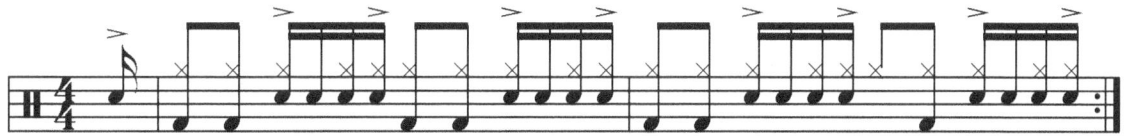

487.

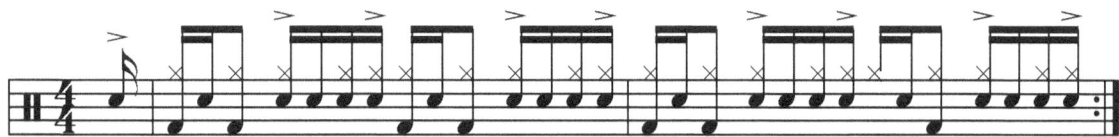

Again the recurring Bernard Purdie figure creeps in, making these grooves meaty and relentless. You can also start to open the hi-hat ever so slightly to get the quasi-open hi-hat mini-barks on the upbeat sixteenth notes. You can achieve this by tapping eighth notes with your left heel on the heel plate of the hi-hat stand and lifting your leg ever so slightly to let the hi-hat open just a tiny bit in the desired places.

488.

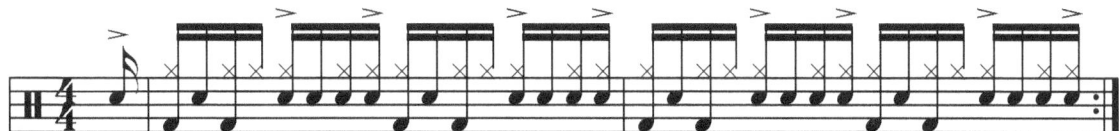

BACKBEATS

489.

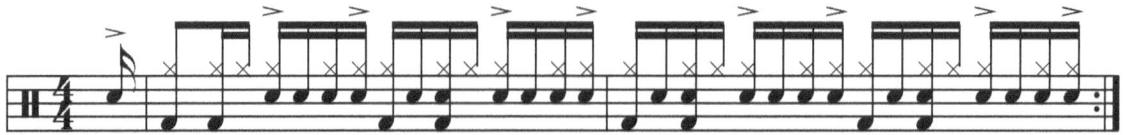

490.

491.

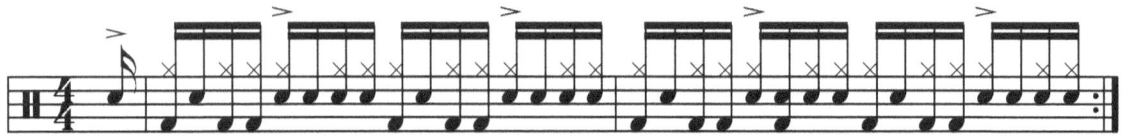

492.

Again, you can apply the "Cold Sweat" rhythmic structure.

493.

BACKBEATS

Now you can change up the right-hand rhythm while keeping the four consecutive notes on the snare.

494.

495.

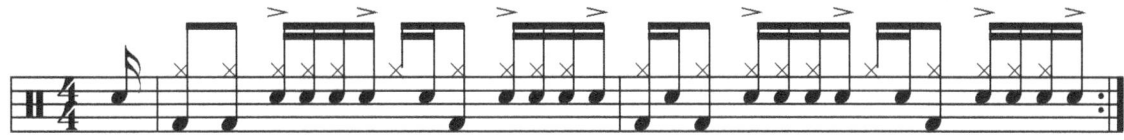

496.

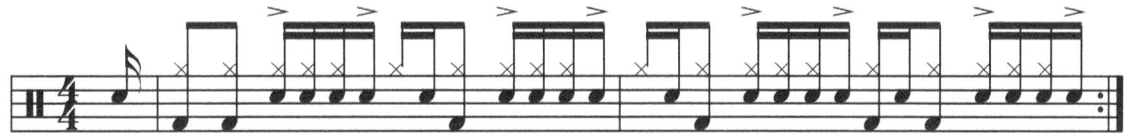

You can also mess with the rhythmic structure.

497.

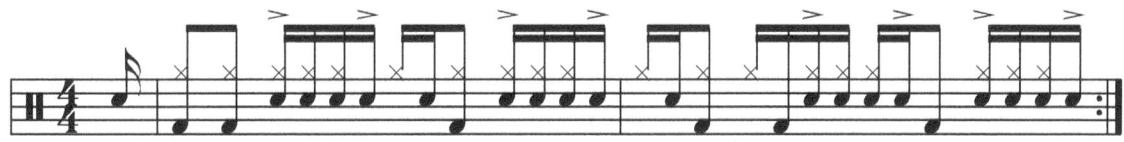

Here's some that keep three consecutive notes in the left hand while simplifying the right.

498.

499.

BACKBEATS

Again, we can play with the rhythmic structure....

500.

Also three consecutive snare notes works great with the Bernard Purdie right-hand rhythm as well.

501.

Now let's look at some of the things we can do in the right hand to ornament the backbeat. The following utilizes three consecutive notes in the right.

502.

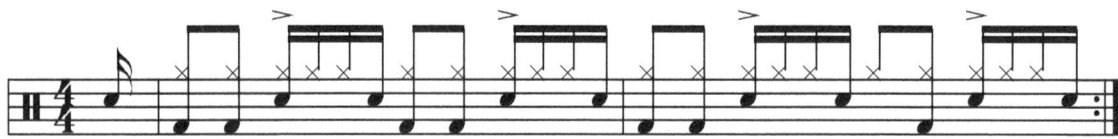

I've seen Zigaboo use these next ideas time and time again, and they're always super funky.

503.

504.

Change the rhythmic structure...

506.

BACKBEATS

You can also add in some chatter notes.

506.

This works great when you go to the bell as before.

507.

508.

Change the rhythmic structure…

509.

You can experiment with four consecutive notes on the hi-hat with the right hand as well. These can be very useful.

510.

Add in chatter notes.

511.

BACKBEATS

Three consecutive notes in the left hand works great as well.

512.

Alternate between 3 and 2 chatter notes with the left hand.

513.

So now let's step back a little. Check this out... if you play ex. 508 into 509, you have a four-bar phase with a change of rhythmic structure as a fill at the end. Add a build in dynamics (crescendo), and you have a walloping finish to a section of a tune.

514. AUDIO ONLY

Bass Drum Chatter Notes

Next we can experiment with adding bass drum notes after the backbeat. We can call these "bass drum chatter notes" or, as I referred to them in my previous book, "bass drum after beats." These are notes on the bass drum that follow the snare drum backbeat with a sixteenth note on the bass drum immediately following the snare. We've seen a couple of these creep up in previous examples, but let's examine further .

Let's start with varying our most basic example…

515.

516.

BACKBEATS

You can also combine snare and bass chatter notes.

517.

518.

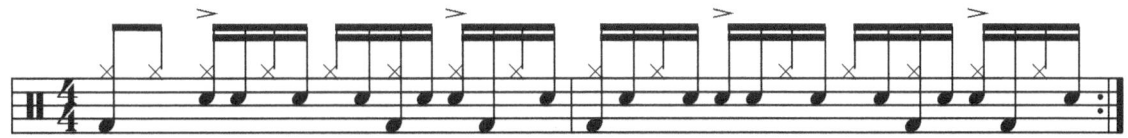

You can put a bass drum chatter note after a snare drum double backbeat. There is plenty more on this concept in *Take It To The Street*.

519.

Make sure to experiment with this concept on your own as well.

To hear the application of the concept of adding chatter notes on the hi-hat, check out the song "Knocker" on my *Groove Alchemy* (Telarc Records, 2010) album.

Experimenting with the Sound of the Hi-Hat on the Backbeat

A lot can be done to vary the sound of the hi-hat on the backbeat. Let's start with leaving out the hi-hat on the backbeat. This concept has been used to great effect by the Rolling Stones' Charlie Watts. He has built his entire style around the notion of leaving out the hi-hat when the backbeat hits. This creates a clean, impacted hit. Let's check out a basic groove á la Charlie Watts.

520.

BACKBEATS

Now we could play this all with the right hand…bring the right hand down to the snare. This would allow you to play the cowbell part to "Honky Tonk Women" with your left hand on a cowbell to the left of your hi-hat. The original cowbell part has tons of variations; this is just a brief example.

521. **"Honky Tonk Women"** approximation, Rolling Stones 1969, drums: Charlie Watts, c. 119 bpm.

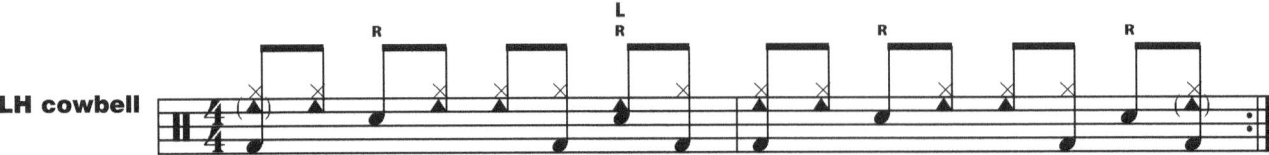

Zigaboo has inadvertently used this concept as well. In his groove to "Cissy Strut," since he is playing both hands on the hi-hat, when the right comes down to the snare for the first backbeat, it is exposed with no hi-hat. Remember that "Cissy Strut" is coming from a two hands on the hi-hat sixteenth-note groove.

522.

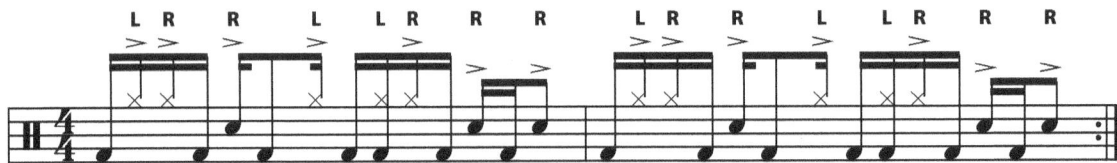

The missing hi-hat note on the backbeat happens on any of these types of two-handed sixteenth-note grooves.

523.

All this being said, if you listen closely, you can hear Zig actually add in the hi-hat notes occasionally with the left hand on the hi-hat. This can be useful in many instances as well.

524.

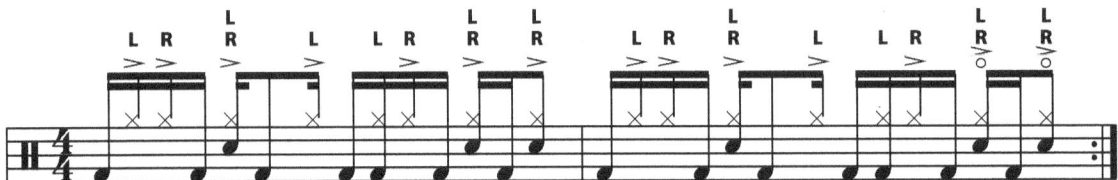

BACKBEATS

In addition to leaving out the hi-hat on the backbeat, you could use the concept of adding an open hi-hat on the backbeat as well. Check out the groove to "Funky Miracle." Remember that the basic idea for this groove comes from the groove to "Cissy Strut." Zig just took the hands from the hi-hat down to the snare and played the open hi-hats to accompany the backbeat. Once you understand "Cissy Strut," you should be able to learn "Funky Miracle" fairly easily.

525. "Funky Miracle" The Meters *Look-Ka Py Py* 1970, drums: Zigaboo Modeliste, c. 96 bpm.

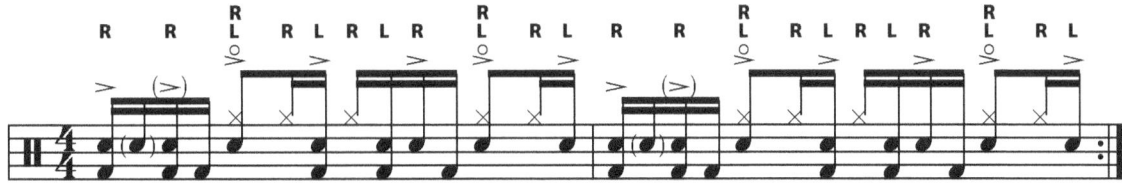

You could also play a crash on the backbeat.

Check out these grooves…

526.

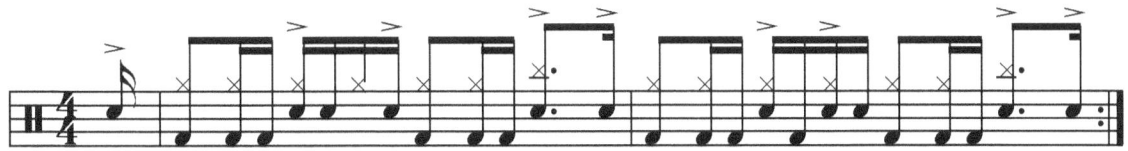

527.

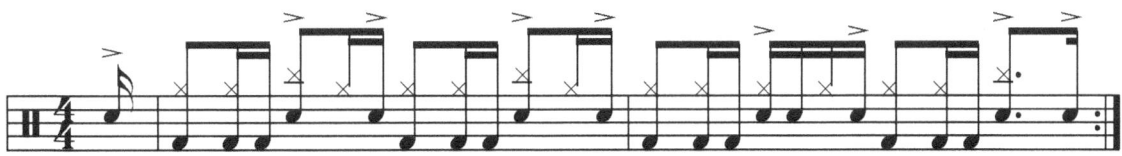

Let's get back to our original simple groove. You could add a crash on the last backbeat of a two- or four-bar phrase for variation.

528.

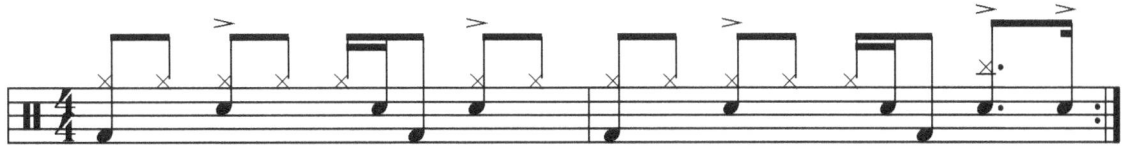

You could add accents to the exposed hi-hat notes to add intensity. I've talked about this in more detail in the "Inflecting and Varying the Groove" section of *Take It To The Street*. The accentuation of these notes was originally caused by compression added to the drums in the studio. Compression makes the softer notes louder and the louder notes softer…so the dynamics of the track are "compressed." Being a softer voice in the kit, when the hi-hat is exposed by itself, compression "accents" the exposed notes. You can hear this a lot in hip-hop and especially in John Bonham's groove to "When the Levee Breaks." To approximate this very cool effect, we can accent the exposed notes on the hi-hat ourselves .

BACKBEATS

Check out ex. 528 with the added hi-hat accents. In my opinion, this subtle detail makes this example groove even harder. Throwing in an accent on the snare on the last sixteenth note of the bar helps add some forward motion as well.

529.

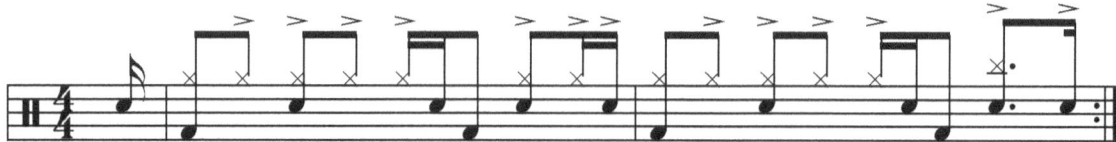

Flamming the Backbeat

Now let's check out adding flams to the backbeat. You can bring the right hand down from the hi-hat to the snare to play a flam. I usually play the right hand as the grace note and the left hand as the accent.

530.

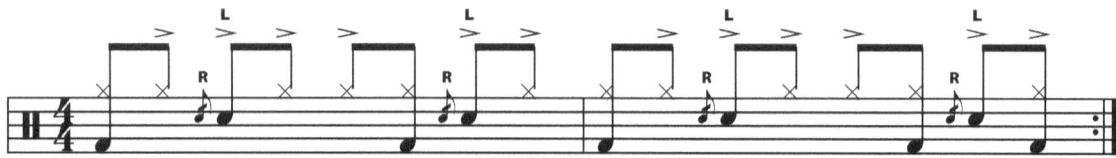

You can also play with both hands on the snare.

531.

Here's one of my favorites that I've "borrowed" from Johnny Vidacovich. Notice the double backbeat and the bass drum chatter notes.

532.

BACKBEATS

Let's check out how John Bonham used flams and crashes on the backbeats of his groove to the middle section of "How Many More Times" from the first Led Zeppelin record.

533. "How Many More Times" middle section at 5:47, Led Zeppelin *Led Zeppelin* 1969, drums: John Bonham, c. 95 bpm.

Let's also take a look at how Zigaboo used flams in his groove to "Africa" from the Meters' album *Uptown Rulers: The Meters Live On The Queen Mary*.

534. "Africa" live version, The Meters *Live On The Queen Mary* 1975, drums: Zigaboo Modeliste, c. 94 bpm.

Note the similarities in these two grooves. We've discussed earlier some of the similarities between Zig and Bonham. They were both born in 1948 and hit the scene at the same time (both of their first records came out in 1969). They both had been into and influenced by a lot of the same music, i.e. early Fats Domino and Little Richard with Earl Palmer (New Orleans) on drums, the drummers of James Brown (namely Clyde Stubblefield), Motown ,and many recordings with Bernard Purdie. John Bonham toured with Tim Rose in 1968. Bernard Purdie played on Rose's self-titled record in 1967. There's a great rare picture of Bonham with his arm around Professor Longhair (the legendary New Orleans piano genius) from a Led Zeppelin record release party in New Orleans. Zep hired Fess to play the party. They loved New Orleans music. Zig played with Fess. Bonham loved Fess. Again, to me there's no coincidence that I find similarities in Bonham's and Zig's playing.

BACKBEATS

Getting Different Sounds with the Backbeat

There are plenty of ways to get different-sounding backbeats as well. You can of course change snare drums, but there's also ways to get different-sounding backbeats out of the same snare drum. In this section I will play the same basic groove for each example, but will change the sound of the backbeat…sometimes subtly, sometimes drastically. I will use the same snare (my signature titanium-shell 4.5x14 snare drum) throughout. I'll change the tuning, muffling, and attack, and try different sticks, brushes, and blasticks, all the while using the same drum with the same heads and snare wires to get different sounds.

Let's start with a light, crisp backbeat á la the drummers of James Brown. James Brown's drummers usually played traditional grip, tuned very high, and played fairly lightly (by today's standards).

That type of backbeat sounded like this…

535. AUDIO ONLY

You could play that closer to the edge for a ringier sound.

536. AUDIO ONLY

Now let's get into some different sounds. Rim shots are very effective. You can get different-sounding rim shots depending on how much stick you leave past the rim as it hits the head. I tend to gravitate toward playing matched grip when I'm playing lots of rim shot backbeats. That's just my personal preference. I feel like gravity is on my side when playing backbeats with matched grip. That being said, Stewart Copeland and Steve Jordan both get atomic backbeats with traditional grip. It's all a matter of preference. Here's a full-sounding rim shot with plenty of stick on the head.

537. AUDIO ONLY

Now if you pull your hand back and play with less stick on the head, you get a higher-pitched rim shot. You can also grip the stick tighter for more of a smack.

538. AUDIO ONLY

You can dig the stick into the head, leaving the stick pressed into the head after impact. This gives a deader, thuddier-sounding backbeat.

539. AUDIO ONLY

Now we can get into the wide world of cross sticks (or rim clicks). You can get thousands of different cross stick sounds. You can change the sound of your cross stick by where you place the back end of the stick on the head, how much stick you let extend past the rim, the position of the stick on the head, the size of the stick you are using, and whether you play with the tip end or butt end forward.

Here are just a few examples.

Butt end forward, lots of stick on the head, only a little bit extending past the rim, 1 o'clock position.

540. AUDIO ONLY

Butt end forward, lots of stick on the head, only a little bit extending past the rim, 3 o'clock position.

541. AUDIO ONLY

Butt end forward, not as much stick on the head, more stick extending past the rim, 1 o'clock position.

BACKBEATS

542. AUDIO ONLY

Butt end forward, not as much stick on the head, more stick extending past the rim, 3 o'clock position.

543. AUDIO ONLY

Front end forward, lots of stick on the head, only a little bit extending past the rim, 1 o'clock position.

544. AUDIO ONLY

Front end forward, lots of stick on the head, only a little bit extending past the rim, 3 o'clock position.

545. AUDIO ONLY

Front end forward, not as much stick on the head, more stick extending past the rim, 1 o'clock position.

546. AUDIO ONLY

Front end forward, not as much stick on the head, more stick extending past the rim, 3 o'clock position.

547. AUDIO ONLY

Now let's check out some of the other things that are possible with cross sticks. You can bring the right hand down and play a strong flammed backbeat on top of the stick itself, where the left hand plays a cross stick grace note and the right plays the accent on the actual stick.

548.

You can experiment with the placement, position, stick choice, and more to try to get different sounds with this as well.

Now let's try playing grace notes with the cross sticks while the right hand comes down to the snare drum for a strong backbeat. The left hand can serve to muffle the head, or you can lift up the left hand to let the backbeat ring a bit.

549.

550.

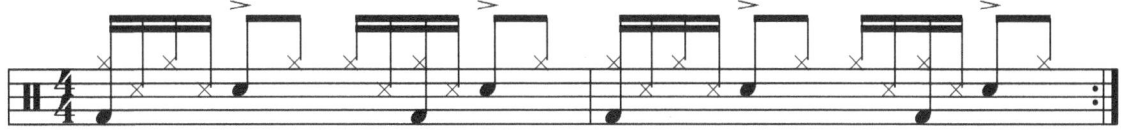

BACKBEATS

551.

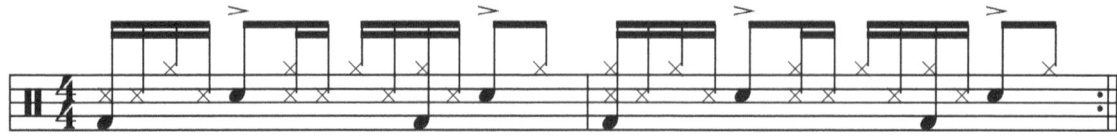

552.

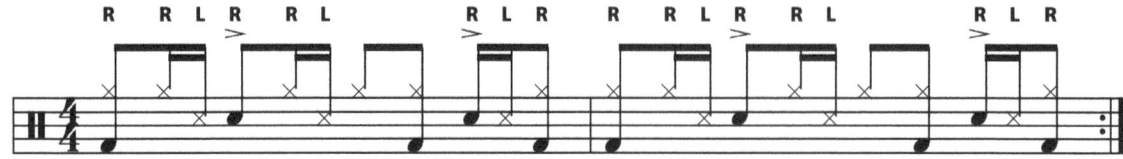

You can also bring the right hand down to the stick to get the cross stick flam that we just examined. Let's add in some open hi-hat notes as well.

553.

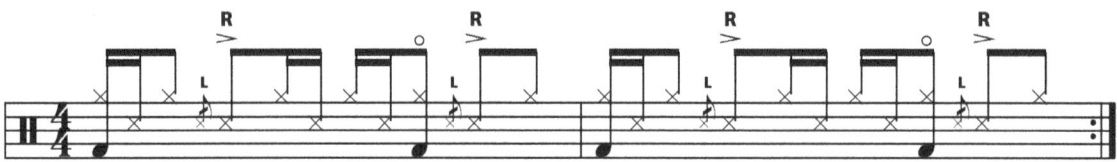

554.

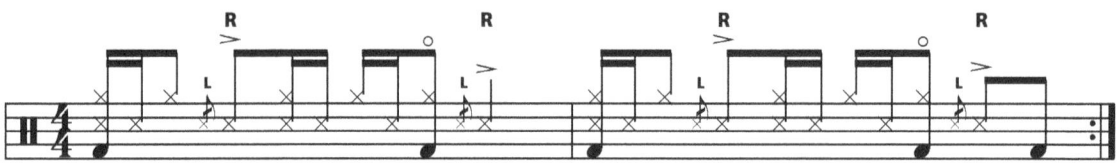

555.

BACKBEATS

Now to give you an example of some of the various sounds you can get with cross sticks, check out this short solo featuring some of what is possible with cross sticks.

556. AUDIO ONLY

Now let's examine some different muffling techniques that can yield some interesting results.

One of the most popular techniques is to put a wallet on the snare…

557. AUDIO ONLY

You could also try a pack of cigarettes, a hockey puck, or a Moongel damper pad as well.

My personal preference is gaff or duct tape with one, two, or three ribbons folded into it. The ribbon creates more mass in a small amount of surface area and is very effective for touring. You can set it and forget it and it doesn't come off while playing or fall off when you pack or move the drum.

558. AUDIO ONLY

For a more subtle technique, some people use a Band Aid on top or underneath the batter head. You could also tape tissue paper to the head with duct or gaff tape to muffle the drum even further.

You could use a Remo O-ring. Steve Gadd has used these to great effect for years.

559. AUDIO ONLY

One thing I've found very useful is to place my pandeiro upside down on top of the batter head. This gives an instant Al Jackson vibe. It helps if the snare is tuned lower for this as well.

560. AUDIO ONLY

If you don't have a pandeiro, you can get a very similar effect with a 12-inch drum head turned upside down on the batter head. This is also easier to play as you don't have to get inside the shell of the pandeiro, which is like dealing with a very high rim that doesn't sound good when you hit it accidentally.

561. AUDIO ONLY

You could also use three sheets of paper lightly taped to the batter head for a similar vibe. This works well because you can still play cross sticks.

For a thuddier sound, you could place a T-shirt or a towel over the batter head.

562. AUDIO ONLY

Now we can start to add additional sounds to the backbeat for different colors and textures. Let's start by adding a tambourine to the backbeat. I usually mount the tambourine to the left of my hi-hat so I can play backbeats with my right while playing the tambourine with my left.

563. AUDIO ONLY

With the mounted tambourine on my left, I can also play other syncopated ideas on the tambourine with my left hand, while I continue to rock the steady groove with my right.

These grooves are similar to some of the grooves in the cross stick section. They also sound great with the left hand on the pandeiro.

564.

BACKBEATS

565.

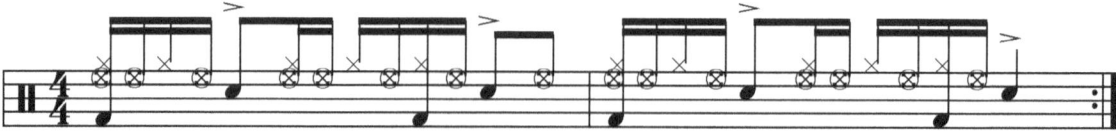

566.

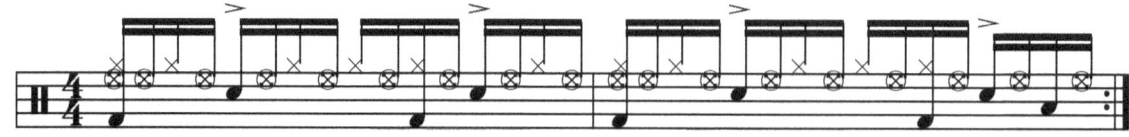

Another effective tactic is to play the floor tom or rack tom on the backbeat á la Al Jackson. I've read that Earl Palmer was actually the first to do this. He was asked by Phil Spector to play the backbeat on the tom along with the snare to fatten it up. You could play it on different backbeats with in a two measure phrase.

567.

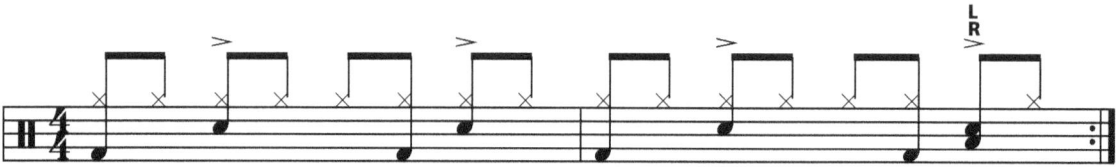

568.

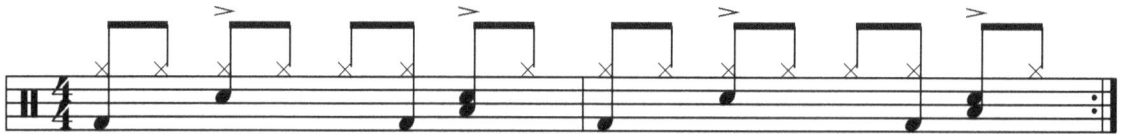

Check out Al Jackson's groove to the intro and choruses of "Still In Love With You." Note that the snare and rack tom are tuned lower and muffled quite a bit.

569. *"I'm Still In Love With You"* **Al Green 1972, drums: Al Jackson Jr., c. 97 bpm.**

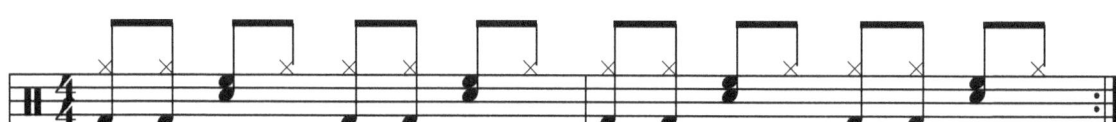

BACKBEATS

Now let's check out Al's very creative groove to the verse. Note that he's getting a snare and rack tom combination on 2 and the cross stick on 4. The upside-down pandeiro or upside-down 12 inch drum head trick we discussed earlier works great for the Al Jackson snare sound, but in this case it's best to use the "three sheets of paper" trick so the pandeiro or drum head hoop don't get in the way of the cross stick.

570. "I'm Still In Love With You" **verse.**

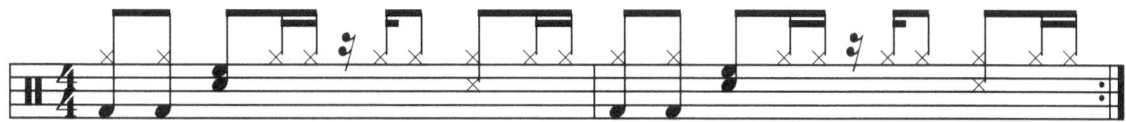

You can add chatter notes on the snare to accompany the floor tom backbeat.

571.

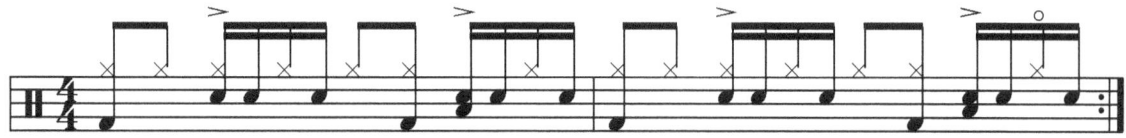

Now let's look at adding some other sounds to the backbeat as well.

You can use a sampler and/or electronic pads to add various sounds to your kit. There are many sampler options out there. I use a Roland SPD-S, which allows me to put in all types of samples and play them at the gig or in the studio. You can sample handclaps, snaps, tambourines, percussion, vocals, instruments, tracks from CDs, sounds from records you've made…basically anything you can think of and play back by hitting a pad.

Once the sounds you want are in your sampler, you can play them with the kit.

So let's check out what it sounds like when you start adding some of these sounds to the backbeat. I set up my sampler to the left of my hi-hat and usually play it with my left hand. When playing the sampler on backbeats, I play the sampler with the left and the snare with the right. Try not to flam these.

Here are some handclaps we created for some of the tunes on Galactic's record *From the Corner to the Block.*

572. AUDIO ONLY

Here are some snaps.

573. AUDIO ONLY

You can play a cross stick with claps, snaps, or tambourine as well. To do this, you play the cross stick with your left hand and bring the right hand off the hi-hat to play the sampler or the tambourine. Check out these grooves.

574, 575, 576. AUDIO ONLY

BACKBEATS

You could even add the bass drum to the backbeat to thicken things up a bit.

577.

This happens all the time in reggae, ska, and rock steady music. Check out this one-drop groove.

578.

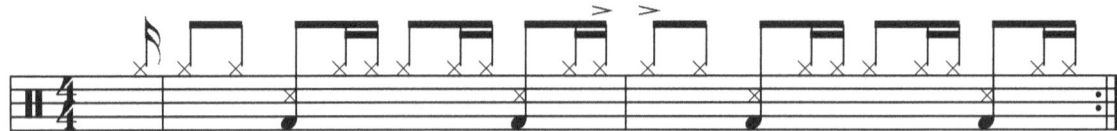

You could play four-on-the-floor, playing the bass drum on all the backbeats, making a driving, relentless groove. Let's try that with the upside-down pandeiro trick (ex.560).

579.

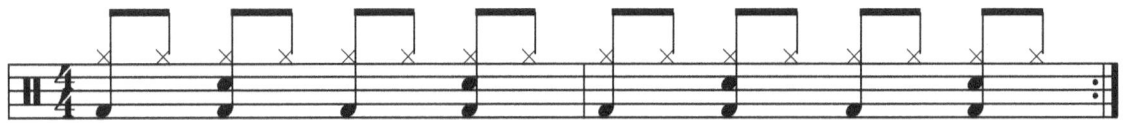

Here's a four-on-the-floor groove that Steve Gadd has used to great effect. Notice the Jabo Starks hi-hat pattern.

580.

Let's check out what happens if we use different sticks or brushes to play the backbeat. I dig the sound of a wire brush playing a backbeat on the snare. The key is to lay as much brush on the head as possible without hitting the shaft of the brush on the snare. This takes some time to develop until you can get a consistent sound every time. You could swish sixteenth notes with the right hand on the snare while the left plays the backbeat.

581.

BACKBEATS

You could also play the right hand on the hi-hat with the right brush wires choked up a bit...

582. AUDIO ONLY...

or the right hand could play on the snare...

583. AUDIO ONLY...

or you could play with any number of different rods on the hi-hat with the right hand.

I also love the sound of a blastick playing the backbeat on a detuned batter head. This sounds great with a rod in the right hand.

584. AUDIO ONLY

Now, we can even turn the snare upside down and play backbeats on the snare side of the snare. The key to not splitting the head is to play out of the drum, or think of lifting the sound out of the drum, much as you would while playing timpani. Don't play into or through it. This way you won't split the very thin and delicate snare-side head. Also try not to hit the snare wires so as not to bend them.

585. AUDIO ONLY

You could scrape the snares and get a scratching sound as well.

586. AUDIO ONLY

This snare sound works great for drum & bass as well.

587.

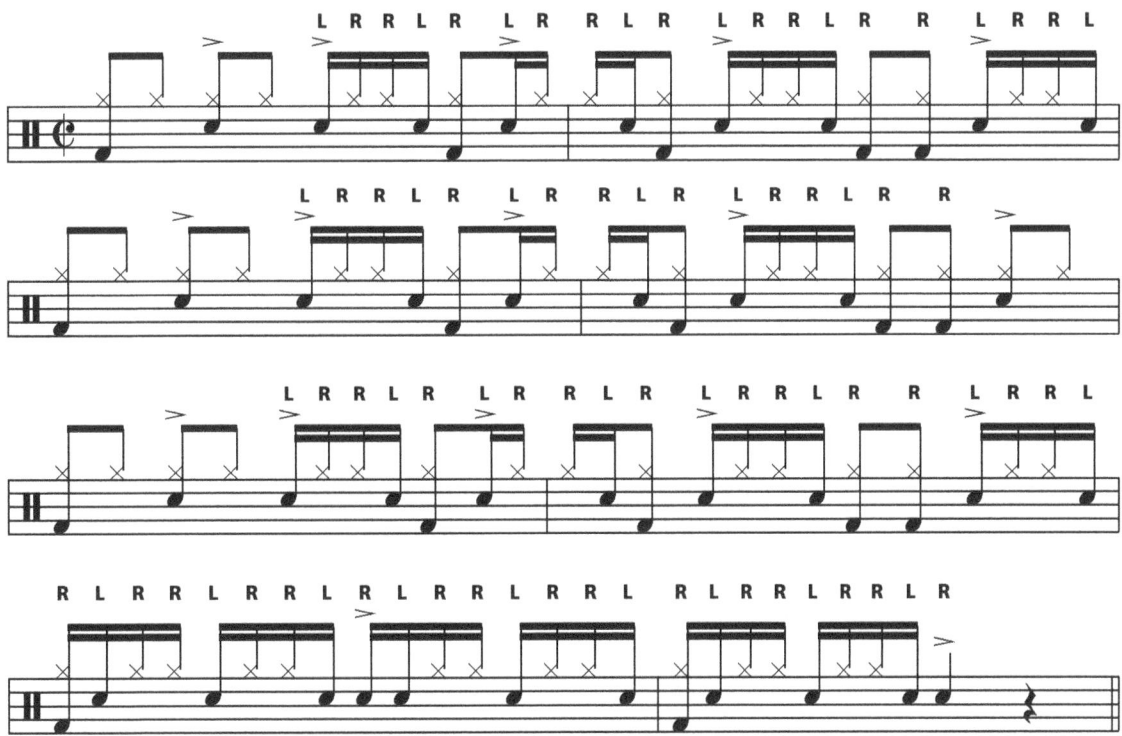

Try experimenting with these ideas and applying them to grooves you already know and grooves you come up with in the future. Also try applying these ideas to some of the different rhythmic structures we've covered.

BACKBEATS

Keeping the Backbeat Present in Fills

I'd like to talk about the concept of playing fills while keeping the backbeat present. Just because you play a fill doesn't mean that you have to forego the groove or even the backbeat. It's possible to play fills and include the backbeat. Usually when I play fills, I like to keep the backbeat or clave or relevant rhythmic structure present. This keeps most of the fills I play related to the groove and the music at hand…a bit of musical continuity, if you will.

Early on in my playing, I would record myself and listen back (I still do this of course). I noticed that certain things I was doing would rush, sextuplet fills in particular. What I did to try to remedy this problem was A) play the groove at hand with a metronome and go into the sextuplet fill, all the while staying locked with the metronome. This helped me "memorize" where the subdivisions should sit at different tempos in different grooves. The other thing that helped my time greatly was B) feeling or internalizing the backbeat even if I wasn't playing it. Feeling the backbeat through everything I did, whether I was actually playing the backbeat or not, greatly helped my playing and helped me learn where everything should sit.

Check out these very simple fills. They start out with the backbeat actually present. See if you recognize some of the stickings these are based on.

588.

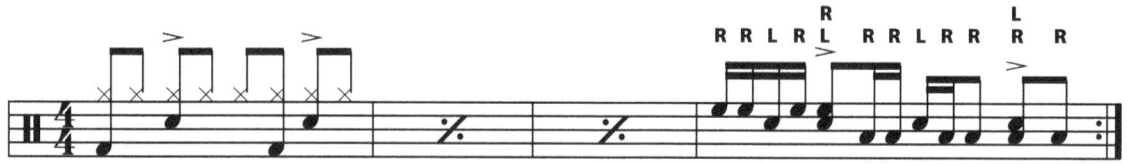

589.

590.

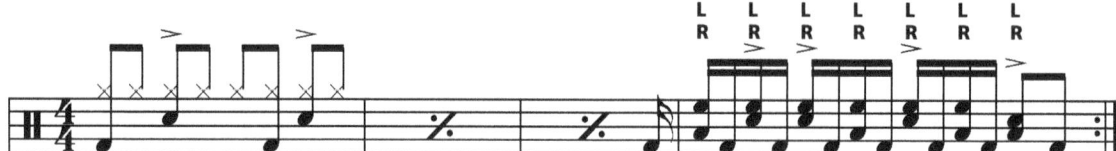

BACKBEATS

Now let's check out these sextuplet fills. These first ones have the backbeat present and will help you learn where to make the sextuplets sit, so when we get into more involved sextuplet fills, they won't rush.

591.

592.

593.

Now try removing the backbeat while still *feeling* its presence.

594.

595.

596.

BACKBEATS

597.

598.

599.

Try working with these concepts for a while. Hopefully they will result in increasing your awareness of the backbeat. Try playing some of the fills you already know while feeling the backbeat underneath or within what you are playing. Try thinking of fills as just groove variations. Try to make your fills just as grooving and locked in as the beats you are playing. In time, this should improve your groove immensely.

PLAY-ALONG
DRUM CHARTS

GROOVE ALCHEMY

PIE-EYED MANC

600. MINUS DRUMS

POT LICKER

601. MINUS DRUMS

ROOT CELLAR

602. MINUS DRUMS

UP TO HERE

603. MINUS DRUMS